LAS VEGAS

BY
JULIE MUNDY

Produced by
Thomas Cook Publishing

Written and updated by Julie Mundy

Original photography by Ethel Davies
Original design by Laburnum Technologies Pvt Ltd

Editing and page layout by Cambridge Publishing
Management Limited, Unit 2, Burr Elm Court,
Caldecote CB3 7NU
Series Editor: Karen Beaulah

Published by Thomas Cook Publishing
A division of Thomas Cook Tour Operations Ltd

PO Box 227, The Thomas Cook Business Park,
Unit 18, Coningsby Road,
Peterborough PE3 8SB, United Kingdom
E-mail: books@thomascook.com
www.thomascookpublishing.com
Tel: +44 (0) 1733 416477

ISBN-13: 978-1-84157-603-9
ISBN-10: 1-84157-603-4

Project Editor: Linda Bass
Production/DTP Editor: Steven Collins

Printed and bound in Spain by: Grafo Industrias Gráficas, Basauri

Cover design by: Liz Lyons Design, Oxford.
Front cover credits: Left © Skye Ellen, Index Stock Imagery, Photolibrary.com;
centre © Walter Bibikow, Index Stock Imagery, Photolibrary.com;
right © Brown Bruce, Workbook Inc, Photolibrary.com
Back cover credits: Left © Jon Arnold Images, Photolibrary.com;
right © Brian Hamilton, Alamy

C o n t e n t s

KEY TO MAPS

★   Start of tour

(215)   Road number

Introduction

Las Vegas is the ultimate city of excess – a 21st-century city, where you can take a global journey through time and space just by walking a few short miles of the Las Vegas Strip. No other city can offer you ancient Rome, Paris, Venice, medieval England, Hollywood or the Far East, all captured within the largest and most luxurious hotels in the world.

Vegas has roots in the Old West

When people think of Las Vegas, many envision European-style resorts with glamorous titles such as Bellagio, the Venetian or the Monte Carlo, while others just see glittering façades over a disorderly gambling town. Gaudy or refined, fairytale or fake, Las Vegas is recognised the world over for its imposing neon architecture, ostentatious showmen and no-limits gambling, described by the *Los Angeles Times* as 'the last great mythic city that western civilisation will ever create'.

The city's attraction is evident in its visitor statistics. With over 127,000 hotel rooms and nine million square feet of convention space, Las Vegas is a leading tourist attraction in the United States, with a county gaming industry worth over $8 billion a year.

With more hotel rooms than Orlando or Los Angeles, over 37 million visitors are seduced by Las Vegas each year. Contrary to popular belief, the city has a greater attraction for tourism than for gamblers. The economic impact of all these wide-eyed visitors exceeds over $33 billion, with the citywide attractions now overtaking the gaming tables for tourist appeal. Compare Las Vegas with other gaming cities. Atlantic City on the east coast may achieve identical annual gaming revenues, but it only holds onto its average visitor for eight hours, while Las Vegas can attract you for days on end.

Its luminous enticement also ensures that 80 per cent of those who visit Las Vegas will return. Desert devotees have come back year after year to see the city evolve: from a scattering of gambling rooms and dude ranches in the 1930s, to the growth of the

Las Vegas has been famed for gambling since 1931

Las Vegas Strip in the '40s, the glamour of the city in the atomic era of the '50s, through to the swinging '60s and beyond.

In the 1990s, the Strip underwent a new construction boom, with the creation of themed hotels such as Treasure Island, with its own bay and pirate-ship battle, and the tropical paradise of Mandalay Bay, followed by the glorious cityscapes of New York, Paris and Venice. Now, we can witness the era of the mega-resort, with billion-dollar creations such as Bellagio and Wynn Las Vegas.

From a small oasis within the desert mountains, Las Vegas has grown to fill the whole valley. It is the fastest-growing metropolitan economy in the USA, and the state cannot build new roads, houses and schools fast enough for its eager residents. As for its visitors, seduced by A-list headliners, Hollywood celebrities, fine dining and entertainment, it is no wonder that millions of people return to Las Vegas every year.

To add to the attractions of Las Vegas, not far beyond the glitter you have southern Nevada, Lake Mead, the Hoover Dam and the Grand Canyon. Breathtaking national parks, in a state that encompasses pioneer territory, the Old West and Native American ancestry.

A southbound view of the Las Vegas Strip

The city of Las Vegas

This city is far more than the Las Vegas Strip. Many package holidays transport you directly from the airport to the Strip, and it is also the first area you will encounter on the long desert drive from Los Angeles; but if this is all you experience, then you really have missed Las Vegas.

Downtown Las Vegas, the Hoover Dam and the Grand Canyon – the creations of man and nature – can often remain unseen. With the Strip being so enticing, it is hard to imagine there is more beyond the neon.

The Las Vegas Strip
The area of Las Vegas Boulevard running from Mandalay Bay to Charleston Boulevard (just beyond the Stratosphere Tower) is known as the Strip. Over the years this road has had several names, from the Arrowhead Highway to the Salt Lake or Los Angeles Highway, before it was christened Las Vegas Boulevard South. It was

nicknamed The Strip by police Captain Guy McAfee, who owned the Pair-O-Dice club on this highway before it was populated by casinos.

Downtown
North of Charleston Boulevard is Downtown Las Vegas. It's not recommended that you walk these areas unless you are in the heart of Fremont Street between Main Street and Las Vegas Boulevard. This is the original casino centre, where Las Vegas first developed. It is now a pedestrianised area, and home to the spectacular Fremont Street Experience.

How to see Las Vegas
The Strip is easy to walk around, although during the summer your main obstacle may be the heat. The Strip has six lanes of busy traffic, but offers wide pavements, several crossing points and bridges for pedestrians, while downtown Fremont Street is completely free of traffic.

Some hotels also have moving walkways into their entrances, and there are elevators and escalators servicing the bridges over the Strip, which even the keenest of walkers will find themselves using after a couple of days on their feet.

Entertainment capital of the world

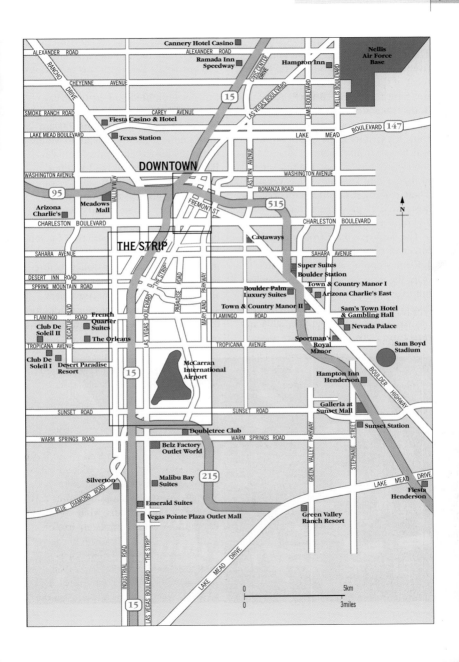

Buses operate from the Downtown Transportation Center on Stewart Avenue, running down the Strip to cover most of the hotels every ten minutes, stopping at the CAT (Citizens Area Transit) bus stops, while off-Strip transfers are also available. The main route for visitors is the Deuce service, which runs from the South Strip transfer terminal, along the full length of the Strip to Downtown Las Vegas. These striking silver double-decker buses hold 97 passengers and run 24 hours a day.

The Las Vegas Strip trolley runs every fifteen minutes from 9.30am until 1.30am, stopping at the major hotels from the Stratosphere to Mandalay Bay, but to avoid the traffic, the Strip also boasts four monorail services. The new Las Vegas monorail opened in 2004 and runs from 7.00am until 2.00am along

the whole length of the Strip from the MGM Grand to the Sahara. While you can buy single tickets for this service, it's far more economical to buy 10 rides at a time, or unlimited one- or three-day passes. Other monorails operate between Mirage and TI, from 9.00am until midnight, from Bellagio to Monte Carlo (24 hours) and from Mandalay Bay, through Luxor to the Excalibur (24 hours).

Las Vegas also has an abundance of taxicabs. They can be found queuing outside the main entrance of most hotels, but the valet must call them over for you. Most taxis will cost more than the MAX monorail, buses, or Strip trolleys before you even start your journey, but they will always be faster and more convenient. Taxi drivers are also great tour guides for the city and can recommend many shows or attractions.

Downtown Fremont Street, the original casino centre

Rental cars can be booked at the same time you arrange your travel plans. If you are already in Las Vegas, the easiest way to hire a car is through your hotel. There are also many rental depots at the airport, but you can face long queues regardless of any previous booking. If your stay is only in Las Vegas, a rental car is not necessary. The Strip is often so clogged with traffic, it is easier to walk or take the monorail system. Taxi drivers know all the back entrances to all the hotels to avoid congestion, and unless you know the same routes, a car may not be worth the expense.

Downtown, the Fremont Street area is pedestrianised and safe for tourists, but it is not recommended that you stray too far from these streets, particularly at night. A Downtown trolley runs from the Downtown Transportation Center on Stewart Avenue and Casino Center Boulevard every 30 minutes with stops that include Fremont Street.

There are many citywide attractions beyond the Strip and the Downtown area, but even some hotel attractions are easy to miss – the establishments are so vast, you can get lost within rows of slot machines and gaming tables before you reach them.

Most hotels have booking desks for excursions and tourist information. Trips to the Hoover Dam or Grand Canyon are plentiful, and whether you see these sights by helicopter, plane or coach, transfers can be arranged from your hotel. Many museums and attractions in the city offer complimentary shuttle-bus services, which will collect you from your hotel if you call ahead.

Tourist traps

As in countless other tourist destinations across the globe, when you walk the Strip or the Downtown area, there will be people working on the street trying to entice you into the casinos. You could be offered free shows, free gaming vouchers, food, drink or anything that may tempt you into their establishments. You will also be offered trips to the Hoover Dam or the Grand Canyon from the street, but although they may be sold by reputable companies, it is advisable to book these trips through your hotel or travel agent, or even before you visit. If you go for the free gifts, that is your choice entirely. You may get a cheap meal, discount vouchers or cheap show tickets as a bonus, but they could waste your time with a lengthy sales pitch.

When you walk the Strip, it is likely that you will encounter people offering you X-rated material and information on prostitutes or strippers, even when you are walking with your family. Prostitution may be legal in Nevada, but that is certainly not the case in Las Vegas, and the best advice is to ignore any leaflets handed to you.

The Riviera was the first skyrise on the Strip

History

1829	Las Vegas ('the meadows') is discovered by Spanish explorers.
1855	The area is settled by William Bringhurst and fellow Mormons.
1905	The Las Vegas town site is founded by Senator William J Clark.
1906	The Nevada Hotel opens Downtown.
1926	The first commercial plane lands in Las Vegas.
1931	Construction begins on the Boulder Dam (later renamed the Hoover Dam). Building was completed in 1935. Gambling is legalised in Nevada and new divorce laws bring tourists in for quickie divorces and wedding ceremonies.
1941	Thomas Hull's El Rancho opens as the first hotel on the Las Vegas Strip.
1942	The Last Frontier, now the New Frontier, opens on the Strip. The Little Church of the West, the first wedding chapel on the Strip, opens

	on the grounds of the Old Frontier.
1944	Liberace comes to Las Vegas to perform on a $750-a-week contract at the Last Frontier.
1946	Mobster Ben 'Bugsy' Siegel opens his Flamingo Hotel on the Strip.
1951	Vegas Vic, the mechanical waving cowboy, is erected outside the Pioneer Club Downtown as a welcome greeting for visitors.
1952	The Sahara Hotel is opened with 240 rooms, the sixth hotel on the Strip.

Aerial view of the Hoover Dam

1955	The Riviera is opened, the Strip's first skyrise. The Moulin Rouge is opened on Bonanza Road and is the first desegregated casino in Las Vegas.
1957	The Tropicana opens.
1958	The Stardust opens, with a record 1,000 rooms.
1959	The Las Vegas Convention Center opens its doors with the World Congress of Flight exhibition. Wayne Newton makes his first appearance on the Strip and remains a headliner today.
1960	The Rat Pack (Frank Sinatra, Dean Martin, Sammy Davis Jr, Joey Bishop and Peter Lawford) hold their legendary summit at the Sands Hotel.
1964	The Beatles perform at the Las Vegas Convention Center.
1966	The reclusive Howard Hughes arrives in Las Vegas, famed for buying out the mob and becoming the largest landowner in Nevada.
	Caesars Palace, the first of the luxurious themed hotels, opens on the Las Vegas Strip. Frank Sinatra marries Mia Farrow in Las Vegas.
1967	Elvis Presley marries Priscilla Beaulieu at the year-old Aladdin Hotel.
1969	Kirk Kerkorian opens the International Hotel on Paradise Road. It is the largest hotel in the world at the time. Elvis Presley makes his stage comeback at the International Hotel and breaks all box-office records for the city.
1972	Jay Sarno, developer of Caesars Palace, opens Circus Circus Hotel & Casino Resort.
1979	The Imperial Palace is opened.
1987	Legendary illusionists Siegfried and Roy are signed to a five-year $57.5-million contract with Steve Wynn at the Mirage.
1989	After a quiet period of development on the Strip, Steve Wynn opens the Mirage, which kick-starts a new era of resort building.

1990	The medieval-themed Excalibur is opened with 4,032 rooms.
1993	The Egyptian-themed Luxor Hotel is opened. Steve Wynn opens his Caribbean adventure hotel Treasure Island. MGM Grand Hotel and theme park is opened with a record 5,005 rooms.
1994	The first Skywalks are built on the Las Vegas Strip.
1995	Downtown is rejuvenated with the opening of the $70-million Fremont Street Experience. The first Hard Rock Hotel is opened on Paradise Road.
1996	The Monte Carlo is opened. The Stratosphere is opened as the tallest structure west of the Mississippi River.

A Vegas-style wedding

	The Sands Hotel is imploded, and plans are announced to replace it with a breathtaking mega-resort, later unveiled as the Venetian, which opens in 1999. Tiger Woods wins the Las Vegas Invitational.
1997	New York–New York Hotel and Casino is opened, receiving over 100,000 visitors a day in its first few days on the Las Vegas Strip.
1998	Bellagio opens on the Las Vegas Strip costing a record $1.6 billion and features the largest choreographed water fountain in the world. This luxurious resort also bans any visitors under the age of 18 unless they are resident in the hotel.
1999	The tropical-themed Mandalay Bay Resort opens on the site of the former Hacienda Hotel. The new resort includes a Four Seasons Hotel on the upper floors. Paris Las Vegas opens on 1 September.
2000	In the largest corporate buyout in gaming history Kirk Kerkorian's MGM Grand Inc. acquires Steve

Wynn's Mirage Resorts, and in the following years MGM also plan to buy out the Mandalay Group.

2001 *Ocean's Eleven* is remade 21 years after the original Las Vegas heist was filmed by the Rat Pack in 1960.

2002 Neonopolis, an 18,580sq m (200,000sq ft) entertainment complex, opens downtown at the Fremont Street Experience.

2003 In a move away from family themed resorts, Treasure Island is transformed into TI, while the Las Vegas Convention and Visitors Authority create a new advertising slogan for the city with the tagline, "What Happens Here, Stays Here." Another Vegas chapter ends when the legendary *Siegfried & Roy* show closes, after illusionist Roy Horn is mauled onstage by a tiger.

2004 Costing $654 million, the Las Vegas Monorail opens, running the full length of the Strip from the MGM Grand, in the southern end of Las Vegas Boulevard, to the Sahara Hotel.

2005 Steve Wynn exceeds his Bellagio price tag to open Wynn Las Vegas, the most expensive hotel in the world, at a cost of $2.6 billion, while Las Vegas celebrates its 100th birthday.

2006 Planet Hollywood Hotel and Casino opens on the site of the 40-year-old Aladdin Hotel, while the Hotel San Remo is transformed into the world's first Hooters Hotel and Casino and groundbreaking begins on Las Ramblers, a $3-billion mega-resort developed by actor George Clooney and nightclub developer Rande Gerber.

2007 Resort owner Steve Wynn begins construction on the $1.4-billion hotel Encore and the development company Las Vegas Sands opens the multi-billion resort Palazzo. Hotel construction in this year exceeds $4 billion, resulting in over 4,000 new hotel rooms and an additional 44,500sq m (480,000sq ft) of convention space, with more billion-dollar resorts to follow.

Contrary to Hollywood legend, Las Vegas welcomed gamblers, gangsters and Hollywood celebrities long before Ben 'Bugsy' Siegel swung open the doors of his Flamingo casino in 1946. This notorious wiseguy is often credited as the founding father of Las Vegas, but Ben Siegel was certainly not the first to break ground in the oasis.

The desert area known as Las Vegas, or 'the meadows', was originally discovered in 1829, located just off the old Spanish trail from New Mexico to California, which had been frequented by travellers and explorers since the 1700s. The first detailed maps of the area were created by Captain John C Frémont, who described two warm springs in his journal, writing: *'The taste of the water is good, but rather too warm to be agreeable; the temperature being 71 in one and 73 in the other. They, however, afforded a delightful bathing place.'*

The area was later home to a small Mormon community, but without the luxury of air conditioning the missionaries were unable to withstand the desert temperatures and left within two years, leaving behind an abandoned fort, which is still preserved today as a state historic park.

The city was officially founded in May 1905, during an historic auction in which railroad tycoon William J Clark sold lots on his new Las Vegas town site. A year later, the Hotel Nevada was opened Downtown and still stands

today as the Golden Gate Hotel and Casino.

Although drinking and gambling were both prohibited in the early 20th century, visitors and residents frequented Block 16, an area designated by Clark's railroad company for the consumption of liquor. Prohibition laws were also ignored to celebrate construction of the Boulder Dam, which brought a promise of work to an economy crippled by the Great Depression.

In 1931, gambling was legalised throughout Nevada. As state officials had already closed down Block 16, in fear that it was corrupting Las Vegas residents, legitimate casino owners began developing new establishments two blocks away around Fremont and Second Street. The Apache and El Cortez were some of the first to appear during an unprecedented neon boom, which created the Downtown area known, for its gaudy façades and sparkling illuminations, as Glitter Gulch.

Starting in 1935, this new city was appropriately promoted with Helldorado, a yearly festival that featured a street rodeo, competitions and carnival parade. But new developments outside town changed the city landscape forever.

According to legend, Thomas Hull, a hotel owner from California, visited Las Vegas in the late 1930s to look for new property. His car overheated a few miles south of the city and, amazed by the volume of traffic heading downtown, he decided to build his hotel outside the city limits. Thomas Hull's El Rancho opened in 1941 and became the first hotel on the Las Vegas Strip. It was followed a year later by the Last Frontier, but was shortly eclipsed by the Flamingo, a lavish development that ushered in the future of glittering, conspicuous resorts. These included the Hacienda, which began its own Hacienda Airlines to fly customers into Vegas. These glamorous resorts have evolved over a period of 50 years to become the Las Vegas of today – luxurious surroundings within a paradise for all ages.

Opposite: El Cortez in Glitter Gulch
Above: The luxurious Mandalay Bay and Four Seasons Hotel occupy the site of the former Hacienda

Nearly 90 per cent of visitors gamble

Governance

Residents of California can elect actors and action heroes such as Arnold Schwarzenegger as State Governor. But only in Las Vegas could they elect a former Mafia attorney as Mayor.

In its brief history, Las Vegas has been governed by several factions – from the gun laws of the Old West, to the days of mob rule and corruption in its early days as a tourist attraction, to the corporate ownership that dominates the city today.

When the city was founded in the early 20th century, residents had little regard for the law or those that enforced it upon them, and the same men that provided the rail lines or city resources, such as water and electricity, also controlled politics. Although drinking and gambling were prohibited at the beginning of the century, county officials and politicians seemed to be immune from prosecution and joined the residents in Downtown Block 16, where a blind eye was turned to their indulgence in drinking, gambling and prostitution.

An early Justice of the Peace was a blacksmith named Jacob Ralph, who would use his business premises as a courtroom. The fine for any misdemeanour usually equated to the amount of money the accused held in his pocket when he was brought before the judge.

The city's second Sheriff, Sam Gay, stands out as a lawman with greater principles. This broad six-footer did not touch alcohol and could break up any fight without drawing a gun, as he preferred to grab the wrongdoers by the scruff of their necks and knock their heads together, then save his target practice for the twinkling new lights in the city.

Today, with over $8 million gained in county gaming revenue, locals claim it is the casinos that call the shots. On average, Las Vegas casinos pay half the amount in taxes that the rest of the country has to surrender, while extra taxes are levied on small businesses and entertainment. The Federal Government is often called to investigate bribes taken by councillors and commissioners from establishments such as strip clubs, while locals claim that the best lawmen they ever had in town were the Mafia.

Throughout the 1940s and '50s, glamorous new resorts began appearing on the Las Vegas Strip. The Flamingo, the Sands, the Desert Inn, the Tropicana, the Thunderbird, the Sahara, the Stardust, the Dunes and the Riviera may have looked like legitimate businesses, but the real ownership and control of these establishments was exerted by Mafia families spread across the whole of the United States.

Surprisingly, the mob was often an attraction for Las Vegas visitors, but during the 1960s government officials began a determined campaign to crack down on organised crime, which started a new era in corporate ownership.

While an aggressive tourism campaign has almost erased the city's unfavourable history, city Mayor Oscar Goodman wants to revive the ghosts of his wiseguy buddies as the city council approved plans to open a downtown mob exhibit – where the Mafia's very own defence lawyer and publicist can finally pay homage to the men who gave him 'juice' in the city.

You never know who might be dealing!

Culture

Las Vegas has its own unique culture. In the 1930s and '40s, as the new city grew, it clung to its roots in the Old West, with Frontier-style hotels and dude ranches. The population boomed with job seekers keen to escape the dust-bowl states and share the prosperity in the West as hopeful workers signed up for construction of the Boulder Dam. The new gambling laws brought in speculators and entrepreneurs, and entertainers soon joined the throng, as showgirls, magicians, singers and dancers auditioned for work in Las Vegas, creating a city with a wide cultural diversity.

The Guggenheim Hermitage Museum

Native Americans were the first settlers in southern Nevada, followed by Spanish explorers, who were the first Europeans to reach the area. The Hispanic influence can be seen today in landscaping, art and architecture but is most evident in the city's name. The French and British followed the Spanish and were soon accompanied by a huge mix of European settlers. Asian and Pacific Islanders began their migration to the area in the 1800s, working as miners, ranchers or labourers, particularly on the expanding railroads. While Europe was threatened by Nazi Germany, Jewish settlers were not victimised by the same religious prejudice and their businesses flourished in Nevada where throughout the 1940s and 1950s many of the new Strip establishments were owned by Jewish investors.

Many African-American entertainers such as Sammy Davis Jr and Nat King Cole performed on the Strip from its early days, but while the Civil Rights movement made great headway in the rest of

The *Fiore di Como* at the Bellagio

The magnificent lobby of the Venetian

the country, Las Vegas was slow to respond. To black entertainers in the 1950s, the city was known as the Mississippi of the West. While they could perform on the Strip, they were not welcome offstage, regardless of how famous they were. As glamorous high-rise hotels grew in the city, a small motel on Bonanza Road changed history when in 1955 the Moulin Rouge became the first desegregated casino in Las Vegas.

Today, Las Vegas is a huge melting pot of cultures and nationalities, expressed in hotels with all-American themes such as New York–New York, in the European-influenced Paris, Venetian and Bellagio, and in the oriental-themed Imperial Palace. Cuisine is offered by award-winning chefs from across the globe, while world-famous entertainers

and performers grace the stages. In 1993 the Cirque du Soleil, a production company that employs talented individuals from over 40 different countries, made its Las Vegas debut with *Mystère*. German-born illusionists Siegfried and Roy were headliners on the Strip, while the famous showgirl revues such as *Folies Bergère* and *La Femme* originated in Paris.

World-famous works of art are displayed in the Bellagio Gallery of Fine Art or the Wynn Collection, the private collection of resort developer Steve Wynn that includes works by Picasso, Cézanne, Van Gogh and Matisse. At the Venetian you can visit the Guggenheim Hermitage Museum, a joint venture under the patronage of the Minister of Culture of the Russian Federation, Dr Mikhail E Shwydkoi.

Las Vegas is famed for its opulent hotel properties, every form of gambling from penny slots to high stakes baccarat, beautiful showgirls, mysterious illusionists, and stunning production shows and headliners, all combining to earn the desert city its title as entertainment capital of the world.

Everybody who is anybody has played Las Vegas: Frank Sinatra and his Rat Pack, Elvis Presley, Liberace, the Beatles, the Stones, the Three Tenors, Tom Jones and Tiger Woods have all headlined in the city along with many others too numerous to name here. Alongside the celebrities, hotels have their own shows, comedy clubs, live music venues, sporting events and convention centres.

The most celebrated productions in Las Vegas are presented by the world-class Cirque du Soleil. Formed in 1984, their shows have been seen by an audience of over 60 million across the globe and feature a cast from forty different countries. Cirque du Soleil currently has four shows resident in Las Vegas. *Mystère, 'O', Zumanity – Another Side Of Cirque Du Soleil* and *KÀ*, plus they recently announced plans for a new production at the Mirage to showcase the musical legacy of the Beatles.

Mystère opened in Treasure Island in 1993 (now known as TI) and has been named eight times as the Best Production Show In Las Vegas. With world-class acrobats, gymnasts and musicians along with high aerial ballets and stunts, *Mystère* is described as the journey of human potential.

In phonetic terms, '*O*' is French for *eau* or water. Showing at the Bellagio, each scene takes place in, on, or

above water, as the stage is set around a pool of water measuring 30 by 45m (100 by 150ft) and 7.5m (25ft) deep. Performers include trapeze artists, divers and synchronised swimmers in a spectacular, which has also been honoured as the Best Production Show In Las Vegas.

Resident in New York–New York, *Zumanity – Another Side of Cirque Du Soleil* has been described as risqué, sensual and alluring, with some very erotic scenes, yet displays the company's unique ability of demonstrating the remarkable capabilities of the human body.

In February 2005, Cirque du Soleil premiered *KÀ* at the MGM Grand, which presents an epic tale of two imperial twins. The show features an impressive cast of 80 performers, with outstanding martial arts, acrobatics, puppetry and a dazzling display of special effects and pyrotechnics.

Caesars Palace recently added the 4,000-seat, $95-million Colosseum to their property where headliners include Celine Dion in *A New Day*, which is produced by Cirque du Soleil's Franco Dragone and Elton John in his acclaimed show *The Red Piano*.

Along with Steve Wynn, Franco Dragone is also the creator of *Le Rêve*, a stunning new production with over 70 world-class

performers, featuring a 3.8-million litre (836,000-gallon) pool surrounded by 2,080 seats all at centre stage.

Las Vegas is also home to huge event centres such as the MGM Grand Arena and the Mandalay Bay Events Center. Added to the city's ever-growing list of showrooms and theatres, your choice for entertainment is endless.

Opposite: The imposing MGM Grand, home to the Arena venue. Below: Caesars Palace has brought headliners to the Strip since 1966

Festivals and events

As well as inviting tourists, Las Vegas attracts over six million convention delegates each year, along with sports fans who come to support golf championships, boxing matches, basketball games and several rodeo events. Since the first resorts began appearing on the Strip in the 1940s, music fans have chosen Las Vegas as the destination to see their favourite singing stars, and the city also plays host to ceremonies such as the Billboard Music Awards.

A home for professional golfers

January
In January 150 drivers compete in the **Laughlin Desert Challenge**, where desert race cars and trucks race from sunrise to sunset in SCORE International Off-Road Racing.

February
If Fremont Street is not lively enough, in February it plays host to the **Las Vegas Mardi Gras**. Other city events include the **Las Vegas International Marathon** and the **Big League Challenge**.

March
Eight men's and women's basketball teams compete in 14 games for the **Mountain West Conference Basketball Championship**, and the Las Vegas Motor Speedway is host to the **UAW–DaimlerChrysler 400 NASCAR** along with the **Sam's Town 300 NASCAR**.

April
Baseball fans meet in Las Vegas for the **Big League Weekend** just before the start of the season. Top cowboys compete in the **Laughlin Rodeo Days**, while Laughlin also plays host to the

Laughlin River Stampede PRCA Rodeo where cowboys compete for over $225,000 in prize money, then the **Laughlin River Run** welcomes over 50,000 bikers for the largest Harley-Davidson motorcycle rally in the West.

May
Las Vegas is the final destination for the **EA SPORTS Supercross Series**, which attracts 40,000 spectators to the Sam Boyd Stadium.

June
Film fans flock to the city for the **CineVegas International**, while high-performance powerboats race along the Colorado reaching speeds of over 217kph (135mph) in **Laughlin River Days**.

July
The Sam Boyd Stadium presents the **Copa Coors Light Soccer**.

September
Top bull riders from the Professional Bull Riders Bud Light Cup tour compete for $100,000 prize money in the **Laughlin**

Shoot Out. The city presents the **Las Vegas Stampede**, while the **Primm 300 SCORE International** takes place off-road on the California–Nevada border.

October
The Las Vegas Motor Speedway plays host to **Las Vegas Bike Week, AMA Superbike Championships**, the **NASCAR Craftsman Truck Series Race** and the **World of Outlaws/NASCAR Winston West Races**. **The Invensys Classic at Las Vegas** sees PGA Tour golfers competing, while the longest hitters play the **Re/Max World Long Drive Championships** in Mesquite.

November
The PDR Bud Light World Championships in Las Vegas see the top 45 bull riders compete for $1.5-million

prize money. The best ropers take part in the **Laughlin Team Roping**, while **Wendy's Three-Tour Challenge** invites teams from the PGA Tour, Senior PGA Tour and LPGA Tour to compete.

December
The PRCA's National Finals Rodeo, the World Series of rodeos, returns to Las Vegas for ten days, while the **Billboard Music Awards** take place at the MGM Grand Garden Arena. NCAA basketball players compete in the **Las Vegas Showdown** while the **Sega Sports Las Vegas Bowl** takes place at the Sam Boyd Stadium, featuring the second selection from the **Mountain West Conference** and the fifth selection from the **Pac-10 Conference**. Finally, end the year watching the city's sensational fireworks spectacular.

The enormous Las Vegas Convention Center, home to many of the city's events

Impressions

It may have been captured in countless Hollywood blockbusters, but even the big screen cannot do Las Vegas justice. This sparkling entity is also impossible to convey in a guidebook. You cannot communicate the sights and sounds, or the feel of the warm desert sun within a few pages. Las Vegas is the ultimate must-see destination.

The Las Vegas monorail

Before you leave

Before you book any flights or make any other travel arrangements, make sure there are hotel rooms available on the dates you wish to visit. Over eighty per cent of the hotel rooms are booked during the week, while the occupancy runs at over ninety per cent at the weekends. This is greatly affected by public holidays such as Thanksgiving or Labor Day, and when special events or festivals are taking place. Las Vegas also welcomes nearly six million convention delegates every year and at times the impact of all these visitors means that there are few rooms available and you could end up paying a room price many times higher than the usual rate.

Hanging around at New York–New York

If you choose to book through a travel agent, or you are travelling as part of a tour, the fixed price you pay will be based on the season and will allow for fluctuations due to other events.

How to get there

Las Vegas is located at the southern tip of Nevada and is serviced by McCarran International Airport, located just south of the Strip. The airport manages over 40 million flights each year, connecting it with most locations within the United States. If you are flying in from overseas, only a few airlines offer direct flights, as most carriers will fly you to a gateway city first.

By car, Las Vegas is 469km (291 miles) east of Los Angeles on Interstate 15, nestled between the California and Arizona borders, and on the Reno-to-Phoenix Interstate 95. From the west coast it's a long desert drive that will take between four and five hours, so ensure that your vehicle is roadworthy for the journey and keep an eye on fuel consumption. Bear in mind that the air conditioning in your car may also affect your petrol usage, and for most of the year you will be unable to make this journey without it.

When to visit Las Vegas

Las Vegas is a year-round 24-hour city. To avoid the crowds, plan your visit away from public holidays, and try to visit during weekdays (Sunday to Thursday). The only days that attractions may be closed are Christmas Day and possibly Thanksgiving.

Las Vegas is warm all year round, but during the summer months between

The star-studded Palms hotel

June and the end of August temperatures can reach well over 38°C (100°F). Peak season runs from April to September, and the best time to visit is at the start or tail end of the season, when Las Vegas will still be very warm. In winter, out of the sunlight or during the evening, there is a marked drop in temperature.

What to wear

The most important item to pack is a pair of comfortable shoes. The Las Vegas Strip is over 5km (3 miles) long, and you will cover vast distances just by visiting the hotels and their attractions. Even if you only cover a third of the Strip, you can get lost in each hotel for hours. The dress code is casual in Las Vegas. In the summer, take shorts, T-shirts and light comfortable clothing. It is advisable to

There are several walkways where you can cross the Strip

cover your skin from the sun, but ensure you apply a high-factor sun cream for any exposed areas. In winter, it is advisable to take a jacket or warmer clothes, particularly for the evening.

Some restaurants or shows may have a formal dress code, so pack something for those occasions. There are many new nightclubs in Las Vegas, and some of these have relaxed dress codes (and admission fees) for women, but stricter rules for men, who may not be allowed in wearing trainers or jeans.

Arriving in Las Vegas

If you arrive by air, try to book your flight to arrive in the evening, so you can get your first glimpse of Las Vegas by night. The city appears so large and luminous you feel as if you are landing right next to the Strip. In true Vegas style, the inside of the airport is filled

with fruit machines. If you arrive between Thursday and Saturday, expect the airport to be busy, particularly in the baggage-claim area. At the time of booking your trip or accommodation, you may be offered transport to your hotel: this will be located just outside the baggage claim, along with taxis and limousine services. One of the easiest and most cost-effective ways to reach your hotel is to purchase a shuttle-bus ticket from one of the many booths in this area, which can take you to any of the Strip or Downtown hotels. Most of these buses offer a return ticket, and you will have to ring and reserve a pick-up shuttle the day before you intend to leave. After a long journey, many flustered passengers easily lose their return tickets for this service, so place them somewhere secure, preferably with your travel documents.

Tipping

From the moment you arrive in Las Vegas – or anywhere in the United States – you will realise that every good service requires a tip. Expect to add 15–20 per cent to your restaurant bill, and unless seating is assigned, pay showroom maitre d's $5–$20 for a good seat. Cocktail waitresses expect $1–$2 per round, and 15 per cent journey fare should be given to taxi drivers. The valet that beckons your cab will also expect a tip for his efforts. $2–$5 per day should be paid for housekeeping on departure, and a similar gratuity should also be paid to tour guides, for valet parking, and for each piece of luggage carried by a hotel porter.

If you are playing card games, roulette or craps, it is good gaming etiquette to tip the croupier after a run of good luck, or to place a bet on their behalf. Card dealers, slot attendants and keno runners should also receive a gratuity.

European splendour at the Monte Carlo Resort and Casino

The Las Vegas Strip

As you drive in from Los Angeles, or arriving from McCarran International airport on Highway 91, you are greeted by the old familiar sign, *Welcome to Las Vegas*. This is the southern tip of Las Vegas Boulevard, the start of the Las Vegas Strip.

Ahead of you, in a sparkling vision of gold, is the Mandalay Bay resort and casino, radiant and imposing, and this is just the beginning. As you drive up between the palm trees you will pass the striking black pyramid of the Luxor, guarded by its gargantuan Egyptian sphinx, the skyline of Manhattan and the Statue of Liberty at New York–New York, then the domineering MGM Grand, Monte Carlo and Planet Hollywood.

With its bright lights, the Las Vegas Strip is an incredible sight – it is no less impressive by day. By night the neon blazes and twinkles, but by day, under a sapphire-blue desert sky, the resorts are even more colourful and vivacious while the neon still glistens under the sun.

Heading up the Strip you see the sumptuous Bellagio, with its magnificent lake and fountain display, and Paris, complete with the Eiffel Tower. Beyond this is the legendary Caesars Palace, an affluent resort fronted by Roman statues, fountains, colosseum and landscaped gardens. After a little ancient history you have a taste of Las Vegas ancestry, with the Flamingo Hotel, the first luxurious resort in a town once steeped in the Old West.

The best way to see the Strip is on foot. Stunning as these resorts appear from the outside, just wait until you see the inside.

You need to give yourself time to explore as many as possible, and you do not have to be a hotel resident to enter. Obviously some areas are reserved for guests, but this is Las Vegas, after all: there are casinos inside and they want to lure you in.

After Paris, another beautiful European city is depicted in the Venetian, which stands opposite the exotic paradise Mirage, with its erupting volcano, and TI, home of the controversial new street show *The Sirens of TI*.

As a city, Las Vegas is always evolving, and the dream resort Wynn stands opposite a grand old resident of Las Vegas Boulevard, the New Frontier. Exhausted from walking, or distracted from driving by the architectural eye candy, you reach the glittering northern point of the Strip. The Stardust and Riviera, two survivors from the fabulous '50s (with the latter being the first high-rise to appear on the Strip), make way for the carnival-themed Circus Circus, then the neon briefly diminishes. With a new burst of radiance from the Sahara, the grand finale is the Stratosphere. At 350m (1,149ft), this tower is the tallest building west of the Mississippi.

Ladies and gentlemen – welcome to Las Vegas.

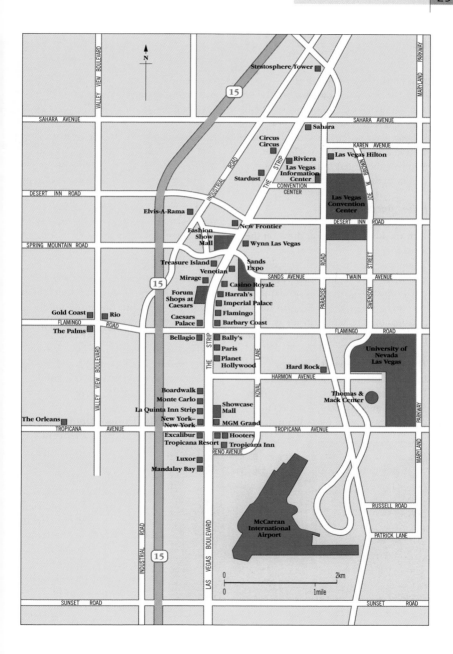

Ten of the best

The Fountains of Bellagio

On its grand opening in 1998, the Bellagio was credited as the most expensive hotel ever built. The hotel is based upon an Italian village of the same name and is set around a 3.4-hectare (8.5-acre) lake, featuring the largest musical fountain display in the world. *See pp60–61.*

Folies Bergère

Las Vegas is renowned for its showgirls, with the longest-running show on the Strip being *Folies Bergère* at the Tropicana. This world-famous show performs twice nightly and features the city's top showgirls. As in similar shows elsewhere in Las Vegas, the girls do perform topless, although the earlier performance is fully clothed. *See pp56–7.*

The Forum Shops at Caesars

In the luxurious setting of Caesars Palace, the Forum Shops contain over 65,000sq m (700,000sq ft) of retail space. As well as an overwhelming selection of shops, the area is famed for its talking Roman statues and breathtaking architecture. *See pp52–3.*

The Fremont Street Experience

With live music, street entertainers and a laser show which covers a four-block section of Downtown Las Vegas. A canopy above the street features 12.5 million LED lamps to create a free animated performance on the largest screen of its kind in the world. *See pp88–9.*

The Grand Canyon

This awe-inspiring natural creation is 445km (277 miles) long and up to 16km (10 miles) wide and 1,600m (1 mile) deep. There are visitor centres on the north and south rims of the canyon as well as many scenic viewpoints. Several tours operate from Las Vegas and the easiest way to see this wonder is by plane or helicopter. *See pp104–9.*

The Hoover Dam

Proclaimed by President Hoover as 'a 20th-century marvel', the Hoover Dam is one of the greatest achievements in the industrial world. Completed in 1935, the Dam restrained the unpredictable Colorado River to meet domestic water needs and provide low-cost hydroelectric power for residents of Nevada, California and Arizona. *See pp112–13.*

The Forum Shops at Caesars Palace

The stunning fountains at Bellagio

bar and restaurants and a fascinating gift shop, which is quite unlike your usual retail outlets. *See pp68–9.*

The Stratosphere

For the best view of Las Vegas and the wildest and highest thrill rides in the city, visit the Stratosphere Tower. You cannot miss this 350-m (1,149-ft) space needle at the north end of the Strip. *See p58.*

Wynn Las Vegas

Everything you could expect, and more, from acclaimed resort developer Steve Wynn. Where lakes, fountains, waterfalls and lagoons meet the ultimate luxury that comes with a $2.7-billion price tag. The most expensive resort in the world, Wynn also boasts the *Penske Wynn Ferrari Maserati* showroom with some vehicles costing in excess of $1 million. *See pp42–3.*

New York–New York

For exciting themed architecture and streetscapes, look no further than New York–New York. The exterior resembles the Manhattan skyline, complete with skyscrapers, the Brooklyn Bridge and the Statue of Liberty among other key buildings, while the interior is based around the city streets. *See pp32–3.*

Star Trek: The Experience

Take a trip on the USS *Enterprise* in this $70-million attraction, just off the Strip in the Las Vegas Hilton. *Star Trek: The Experience* includes the History of the Future museum, with costumes and props from the television series and movies, along with a themed

Wynn Las Vegas, the most expensive resort in the world

New York–New York

The exterior of New York–New York Hotel and Casino is certainly the most impressive display of architecture on the Las Vegas Strip. Designed to recreate the Manhattan skyline, New York–New York is fronted by a 45-m (150-ft) replica of the Statue of Liberty surrounded by a stunning display of city landscapes, including hotel guestrooms located in twelve Manhattan skyscrapers featuring the Empire State Building, the Chrysler Building and the New Yorker Hotel among others.

Sirrico's Pizza

At the foot of the Statue of Liberty there is a 90-m (300-ft) replica of the Brooklyn Bridge, added to many other features including the Grand Central Station Terminal, Ellis Island immigration terminal and a former US Customs House. Following the terrorist attacks on the World Trade Center in 2001, a September 11 tribute was added to the base of the statue when items were placed there in remembrance of those lost in the rescue services.

The final touch is the Manhattan Express rollercoaster, which races around the exterior of the structure and back inside to the Coney Island Emporium. The interior of the hotel is equally impressive, with a 7,800-sq m (84,000-sq ft) casino surrounded by the streets of New York, complete with lampposts and manholes that emit steam. Replica areas include Park Avenue, New York's Financial District, Times Square, Central Park and a Greenwich Village neighbourhood with several shop fronts, bars, cafés and restaurants along the sidewalks.

Within New York–New York you can eat at *America, Chin Chin Café, Gallagher's Steakhouse, Gonzalez y Gonzalez, Grand Central Coffee Company, Haagen-Dazs Ice Cream, Il Fornaio Panetteria, Nathan's Famous Hot Dogs, New York Pretzel* and *Schrafft's Ice Cream,* while the village eateries include *Broadway Burger, Fulton Fish Frye, Greenberg's Deli, Greenwich Village Coffee Co, Hook and Ladder #9, Ice Cream Shop, The Mango Hut, Sirrico's Pizza* and *Times Square to Go.*

Entertainment New York style includes the authentic Irish pub *Nine Fine Irishmen,* with Irish food and drink and unique Irish song, dance and storytelling, *Coyote Ugly,* a saloon bar based on the movie of the same name, the *Big Apple Bar* and the *Bar at Times Square,* with its live duelling pianos. New York–New York's headline attractions are the celebrated comedian Rita Rudner and *Zumanity,* an erotic new production, described as both edgy and provocative, created by the celebrated Cirque du Soleil.

New York–New York's Manhattan Skyline is recreated with towers that are approximately one-third the height of the actual city skyscrapers.

The Empire State Building:
161m (529ft), 47 storeys

The Century Building:
127m (416ft), 41 storeys

The Seagram Building:
91m (300ft), 30 storeys

The 55 Water Tower:
36 storeys

The Lever House Soap Company:
29 storeys

The Municipal Building:
29 storeys, plus a 24-m (80-ft) tower

The AT&T Building:
26 storeys

The Chrysler Building:
152m (500ft), 40 storeys

The CBS Building:
29 storeys

The New Yorker Hotel:
113m (370ft), 34 storeys

The Liberty Plaza:
31 storeys

The Ziggurat Building:
38 storeys

Fronted by the Statue of Liberty, New York–New York is a celebrated example of Las Vegas architecture

Tour: City landscapes

See the world in one city, as the Las Vegas Strip presents famed locations from across the globe. Some hotels have been described as small cities, with accommodation, recreational activities, nightlife and dining all under one roof, but some Strip resorts have taken the theme quite literally, presenting their own version of American and European destinations.

Las Vegas

THE STRIP

Allow one day. Use the Las Vegas monorail to reach some resorts.

1 The Venetian
Your first stop is the beautiful city of Venice, presented in the centre of the Strip with the Venetian Resort and Casino. The architecture is remarkably accurate, presenting Venice landmarks such as the Campanile Tower, St Mark's Square and the Rialto Bridge all connected with replica streetscapes over the Grand Canal, which sweeps through the Venetian in the same way that the water weaves through Venice.

2 The Grand Canal Shoppes
You can spend hours wandering through the Venetian streets visiting world-famous retailers. Grab a coffee or a snack in the food hall, or dine in style at Canalettos or Postrio in St Mark's Square. The Venetian is also famed for its street entertainers, who perform throughout the shopping area, and you may even catch a glimpse of the mysterious Sporatto who stalked the real city streets in the 16th century. Your visit would not be complete without a relaxing ride

on the Grand Canal, escorted by a tuneful gondolier.
Grand Canal Shoppes open daily from 10am.
Gondola rides daily 10am–11pm, Fri & Sat until 11.45pm.
Head south down the Strip.

3 Paris
Just south of the Venetian you cannot miss the Eiffel Tower standing as an architectural marker for Paris Las Vegas. This resort was once the humble Little Caesars, which contained

Paris Las Vegas

only 150 slot machines compared to over 1,700 which are clustered around the feet of the Eiffel Tower today, surrounded by Parisian landmarks such as the Arc de Triomphe, the Paris Opera House and the Louvre, while the guest towers are inspired by the Hotel de Ville.

4 The *Eiffel Tower Experience*

Make sure you take a trip on the *Eiffel Tower Experience* and see the Strip from 140m (460ft) up. Connecting Paris to Bally's next door, Le Boulevard offers a selection of boutiques in a magnificent Parisian setting, where you can sample wines in La Cave or stop for coffee in Le Café Ile St Louis. Located behind the casino in Paris is Le Village Buffet, acclaimed as one of the best in Las Vegas.
Open: daily 10am–1am.
Continue south along the Strip, until you reach the junction with Tropicana Avenue.

Gondola ride at the Venetian

5 New York–New York

Round off the day in New York–New York, the first city-themed resort in Las Vegas and not only acclaimed as the best example of architecture on the Strip but also voted the coolest building in Las Vegas. Stop in at Nine Fine Irishmen and enjoy hearty Irish cuisine, storytelling and real beer, believing you are in Dublin rather than overlooking the Strip. Finally head back into the Big Apple with the Bar at Times Square and finish off the evening with the duelling pianos and riotous sing-along.
Nine Fine Irishmen open for dinner from 4pm.
Duelling piano show times 8pm–3am (weekends until 4am).

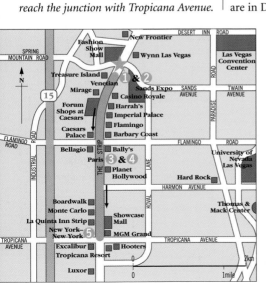

Visit New York City's famous *Studio 54* in the MGM Grand. Once described as the most famous, outrageous and unique nightclub on earth, *Studio 54* has been reborn in Las Vegas. *Open: Tue–Sat 10pm–close.*

All that glitters

Las Vegas has welcomed some of the world's greatest superstars to its showrooms, and many have proved to be as glittering and ostentatious as the illustrious hotels that headlined them. A visit to Las Vegas would not be complete without honouring some of the stars that have played the city and there are many tribute shows, including *Legends in Concert* at the Imperial Palace, a popular tribute to stars ranging from Dolly Parton to Elvis and Madonna. However, for a real glimpse of Las Vegas glamour, there are two stars that cannot be overlooked.

The Liberace Museum

Wayne Newton

Wayne Newton has been performing in Vegas since 1959, when he skipped school for a two-week engagement at the Fremont Hotel with his brother Jerry. Two weeks soon turned into six years and started a series of engagements that continue to this day in the Wayne Newton Theater at the Stardust, where the singer is in residence for 40 weeks of the year. Along with his brother, Wayne had his own TV show at the tender age of 15, and in 1967 Howard Hughes signed him to a contract which saw him perform up to three shows a night at the Sands, Desert Inn and the Frontier, all adding weight to his well-deserved title of Mr Las Vegas.

Liberace

A child prodigy and master of the honky-tonk piano, Liberace first came to Las Vegas in the 1940s, when he was offered a job at the Last Frontier for $750 a week. As his fame grew, Liberace was commanding over $400,000 a week to appear in the city as fans flocked to see 'Mr Showmanship' in his bombastic rhinestone costumes, with his trademark candelabra on top of the piano. Also a

ENTERTAINMENT

Legends in Concert

The Imperial Palace, 3535 Las Vegas Blvd S. Tel: (702) 794 3261 for reservations. Show times 7.30pm and 10.30pm daily (no show Sun). Ticket price includes a drink. Buffet dinner shows are also available.

Wayne Newton

Wayne recently auditioned Las Vegas hopefuls in the television reality show *The Entertainer*. Las Vegas is home to his Casa de Shenandoah Ranch and he performs regularly in the city when he is not on tour.

The Liberace Museum

1775 East Tropicana Ave. Tel: (702) 798 5595. Open: daily 10am–5pm, Sun noon–4pm. Admission is inexpensive and discounted for children and senior citizens.

master chef, Liberace lived, partied and entertained in Las Vegas until 1986 when he gave his last performance at Caesars Palace.

Today, you can see some of his sparkle at The Liberace Museum, just off the Strip on East Tropicana Avenue. Displays include 18 of his 39 pianos, one of which is made out of toothpicks, along with antiques, costumes and cars

belonging to the singer, including a rhinestone-encrusted Rolls Royce. Some of his extravagant costumes weigh up to 80kg (175 pounds) and cost in excess of $300,000.

The museum has recently been refurbished and is operated as a non-profit-making organisation to support the Liberace Foundation for the Performing and Creative Arts.

Legends in Concert at the Imperial Palace

Family entertainment

At first glance Las Vegas looks like an adult playground, but beyond the showgirls and gaming tables the city works hard to maintain its status as a leading tourist destination, with countless attractions to be enjoyed by all the family.

Home to countless thrill rides

Hotels

Las Vegas offers several family-friendly resorts on the Strip including Mandalay Bay, with its *Shark Reef* and beach, the MGM Grand with its lion habitat, and the Stratosphere with its breathtaking views and thrill rides. The Luxor offers attractions that include *King Tut's Tomb*, the seven-storey *IMAX Theater*, motion simulators and the special effects show *Pirates 4D*. Excalibur features the exciting dinner show *Tournament of Kings*, jugglers, entertainers and a court jester's stage in the Medieval Village, along with games, arcades and *Merlin's Magic Motion Machines*. Circus Circus is home to the *World's Largest Permanent Circus* and the *Adventuredome Theme Park*, where, as well as several thrill rides, there are game booths, state-of-the-art video games and a virtual reality zone.

Attractions

Every hotel on the Strip is an attraction in itself and provided you don't exhaust

Beam yourself into *Star Trek: The Experience* at the Hilton

Trapeze acts at Circus Circus Resort and Casino

the whole family by walking, a simple sightseeing trip can last for days. Enjoy the warm climate in the magnificent hotel pools in Las Vegas, or experience the best views of the city from the top of the Stratosphere or the *Eiffel Tower Experience* at Paris, then relax and take a gondola ride at the Venetian.

There are thrill rides, simulated rides, and virtual reality attractions all over Las Vegas. At the Las Vegas Hilton you can journey through time and space with *Star Trek: The Experience*, while older children can brave *Borg Invasion 4D*. Heart-stopping thrill rides include the *Big Shot, High Roller, Insanity – The Ride* and *X Scream* at the Stratosphere, the *Manhattan Express* at New York–New York, *Speed – The Ride* at the Sahara or *Flyaway Indoor Skydiving* on Convention Center Drive. Height restrictions apply on some of these rides.

For arcade games visit the *Coney Island Emporium* in New York–New York, *Carnival Midway* at Circus Circus, or the highly recommended *Games of*

The Gods at Caesars, *Pharaohs Pavilion* at the Luxor or *Gamesworks* on the Las Vegas Strip.

All the family will love meeting the celebrities at *Madame Tussaud's Celebrity Encounter* at the Venetian, seeing the impressive *Auto Collections* at the Imperial Palace Hotel or *The Secret Garden of Siegfried & Roy* and *Dolphin Habitat* at the Mirage. Take a tour of the *Ethel M Chocolate Factory and Cactus Gardens* only 15 minutes away from the Strip or the *Lied Children's Museum*, north of Las Vegas Boulevard.

Many of the family attractions in Las Vegas are free, such as the famed *Masquerade Show in the Sky* at the Rio and world-class street entertainers in the *Grand Canal Shoppes* at the Venetian. Children will be captivated by the talking statues at the Forum Shops in Caesars Palace, then after dark the whole family can enjoy the *Fountains at Bellagio*, the Mirage Volcano, or the Downtown *Fremont Street Experience*.

The fabulous Flamingo

Standing proud in the heart of the Las Vegas Strip stands the shimmering pink Flamingo Hotel. Its ideal location makes the hotel a favourite for Las Vegas regulars and any visitor who wants to absorb a little of Las Vegas history. Originally, all Vegas hotels maintained a Western theme, but in 1946 the arrival of Ben 'Bugsy' Siegel and his fabulous Flamingo Hotel heralded a new age for the city – luxuriant casinos, Hollywood glamour and the infiltration of the Mafia.

Chilean Flamingos

Along with the Flamingo, crime families from the Syndicate to the Cleveland Mob controlled hotels such as the Sands, the Desert Inn, the Tropicana, the Thunderbird, the Sahara, the Stardust and the Dunes.

Legend places Bugsy Siegel as the founding father of Las Vegas, but the

A vintage shot of the Flamingo

Flamingo was actually the third hotel to appear on the Las Vegas Strip, while the Downtown area of the city was already established as a casino hotspot. In true mob style, Ben Siegel lost his life in pursuit of his desert dream as his bosses took revenge for his lavish expenditure on the property.

Today, with the mob long departed, Caesars Entertainment owns the Flamingo Hotel. It pays tribute to Ben Siegel with Bugsy's Bar, named in his honour, which is open 24 hours in the casino.

Over the years the Flamingo has been extensively remodelled and now has more than 3,500 rooms and suites. Nestled within the property is a 6-hectare (15-acre) tropical garden and pool area, which is also home to the Flamingo Wildlife Habitat.

Fine dining is offered at Conrad's Steakhouse, the Flamingo Room, Pink Ginger or Ventuno Ristorante, while casual diners can eat a variety of meals and snacks at Lindy's or enjoy the bountiful Paradise Garden Buffet.

For entertainment, the Flamingo is famed for *Bottoms Up*, which is the only afternoon topless revue on the Strip. At the time of writing recent headliners include Gladys Knight and heavyweight boxing titles, along with *The Second City*, improvised comedy at its best from the company that gave us world-class comedians such as John Belushi and John Candy.

Several Strip hotels offer street entertainment or events, and the Flamingo is no exception, with festivals that include the Wayne Newton Holiday Show.

'EVERY MAN HAS HIS PRICE, OR A GUY LIKE ME COULDN'T EXIST'

Howard Hughes is always remembered as eccentric – a famed recluse, ailed with a variety of phobias, medical conditions and a well-documented obsession with cleanliness. In 1966 the Texan-born billionaire arrived in Las Vegas and took up residence on the ninth floor of the Desert Inn, which he quickly purchased along with the Sands, the Castaways, the Landmark, the Frontier and the Silver Slipper. Taking ownership from the Mafia, these historical business transactions finally shifted the ownership of the corrupt desert city from criminal to corporate.

The Flamingo Hotel today

Tour: The Mafia tour

From the 1940s, crime families from all over the USA invested heavily on the Las Vegas Strip. No wonder it is known as the city the mob built. By the end of the 1970s their reign was over, but these wiseguys created a legend for Las Vegas which continues to inspire movie makers, fascinate historians and add a little more glamour for the tourist trade.

Allow one day. Use the Las Vegas monorail to reach some resorts.

1 The Tropicana

In 1959, Frank Costello survived an assassination attempt. The bullet that was meant to kill the Prime Minister of the Underworld only grazed his skull but rendered him unconscious. When the police searched his pockets they found the first hard evidence of the Mafia's stranglehold on Las Vegas, with a record of the day's takings at the

Tropicana. Start your tour at the Las Vegas Historic Museum, a small but fascinating museum that traces the history of the original hotels that appeared on the Strip. Featuring the largest

The Tropicana

collection of gaming chips in the world, the museum also has a special section dedicated to the Mafia.

The Las Vegas Historic Museum is for over-18s only. Open: daily 9am–9pm.
Head north along the Strip, until you are past the junction with Flamingo Road.

2 The Flamingo

Bugsy Siegel's dream resort was opened in 1946, but with construction costs in excess of $6 million, he repaid that debt with his life. The Flamingo was the third hotel on the Strip, but the first of many mob-owned establishments that would appear over the next few years. Enjoy a cocktail in Bugsy's Bar located inside the Flamingo or take lunch in the Ventuno Ristorante Café and Bar with a fine selection of home-made Italian and Sicilian dishes.

Continue north. Your next stops are either side of Sands Avenue.

3 The Venetian and Wynn Las Vegas

Now the Venetian, the Sands Hotel was owned by a mob collective that included Meyer Lansky, Joe Adonis, Frank Costello and the singer Frank Sinatra, who had a nine per cent stake in the resort. Wynn stands on the site of the Desert Inn, originally owned by Moe Dalitz and the Cleveland Mob. The hotel featured in the first two *Godfather* movies as a Corleone family investment.

Continue north along the Strip until you pass Convention Center.

4 The Stardust

Originally developed by Anthony Cornero Stralla, who mainly operated on the wrong side of the law managing offshore casino boats and profiteering from the prohibition era when he kept the liquor flowing in Las Vegas saloons. After his death, the Stardust had several different owners and soon became a goldmine for the mob, who skimmed huge profits from this resort under the control of the Chicago Outfit. Its colourful history was dramatised in the movie *Casino*, which told the story of Frank 'Lefty' Rosenthal and enforcer Tony 'The Ant' Spilotro.

Go a little further north and cross the road.

5 The Riviera

Chicago bosses such as Sam Giancana once owned the Riviera, where you can stop for dinner in Ristorante Italiano. Reminiscent of old Las Vegas, Martin Scorsese used this restaurant for a scene in *Casino*.

Open: Tue–Sat 5.30–10.30pm.

Retrace your steps back down the Strip to the New Frontier.

6 Ba-Da-Bing

For a lively meal, join the wiseguys at a surprise birthday party for Mr Big at the New Frontier, where a hilarious dinner show turns into an intriguing murder mystery.

Doors open at 6pm, show starts at 7.30pm.

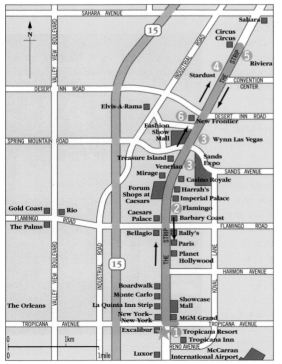

Hotel pools

In the 1940s, when weary travellers made the long journey into Las Vegas from Los Angeles, one of the first sights they saw was the Old Frontier Hotel, which tempted them in with a cooling outdoor pool located right in front of the property on the edge of the highway. Today, the hotel pools are even more irresistible, as Strip resorts boast many beautiful swimming areas and lagoons.

Cool pool at Mandalay Bay

Very often, you will be so overwhelmed by the attractions in Las Vegas, you may not even get the opportunity to spend time in your hotel pool, and some resorts have such an inviting pool area that non-residents are almost green with envy at the amenities they are missing out on. The beautiful pool area at the Mirage is one example. Open to hotel guests only, its tropical setting features two pools, interconnecting lagoons, waterfalls and $^1/_4$ mile of shoreline, surrounded by swaying palms. Relax in the jacuzzis, the *Paradise Café* and *Dolphin Bar* or take advantage of the cocktail service as you lie back in the sun.

The Excalibur Hotel has a very family-friendly pool that can hold up to 800 guests and features a 25-seat spa, waterfalls, water slides, a snack bar and cocktail service, while the Flamingo offers a 6-hectare (15-acre) tropical hideaway, surrounded by vivid pink flamingos and luxurious foliage. There are four pools, including Bugsy's original pool and newer additions with hot tubs, water slides and *The Beach Club* restaurant.

Many pool areas offer cabanas for hire, ranging from basic shelters to luxurious accommodations with dressing rooms, refrigerators, music systems and televisions, as can be found in the Mediterranean pool area at the Bellagio, which offers five pools with hand-carved stone fountains and spas.

Luxury at the Bellagio

Hotel residents can even enjoy a luxurious beach setting at *Ipanema Beach* at the Rio, or the *Beach at Mandalay Bay*. Just off the Las Vegas Strip, *Ipanema Beach* features five pools and five jacuzzis, with waterfalls and spas, surrounded by sandy beaches, while the highly acclaimed *Beach at Mandalay Bay* offers 4.5 hectares (11 acres) of sandy beaches, a wave pool, lazy river, waterfalls, grottoes and lagoons. Enjoy hot and cold meals at the *Beach Bar & Grill*, a snack at the *Surf Café*, or enjoy night-time entertainment on the *Island Stage*, which has recently featured headline acts such as Hall and Oates and Billy Idol.

Throughout the summer months, many resorts host pool parties during the evening, which are sometimes free, while others have a cover charge, which may often include food and drinks. For adults only, there are several poolside nightclubs including *Skin* at the Palms, which features bikini-clad go-go dancers and mermaids, or the *Moorea Ultra Beach Lounge* at Mandalay Bay. For the ultimate all-year pool party try *BiKiNiS* at the Rio, an indoor beach club with underwater performance tanks.

Many resort pools are for hotel guests only, so you will need your room key or pool pass to prove you are resident there. Some hotel pools may close briefly in the winter months, but make sure you take plenty of sunscreen and take advantage of the shelter during the summer.

There are three outdoor pools and a jacuzzi for guests at Caesars Palace

Thrill seekers

If you do not get your kicks in the casino, get your adrenalin racing with some of the world's most exciting thrill rides, all in the city of Las Vegas.

Located at the northern tip of the Strip, the Stratosphere Tower is home to the four highest thrill rides in the world: the *Big Shot, High Roller, Insanity – The Ride* and *X Scream*.

One hundred storeys above the ground, the *Big Shot* fires riders 48m (160ft) upward to a height of 323m (1,059ft). With a greater G-force than astronauts experience on take-off, the journey takes only $2^1/_2$ seconds, but your body still wants to fly upwards after the ride has reached its peak. But do not think it is all over. What goes up must come down, and the ride quickly descends into freefall. Not for the faint-hearted, the *Big Shot* is the highest thrill ride in the world today. Just the aerial

The rides are a long way up at the Stratosphere

view of Las Vegas will be enough to weaken your knees.

Also on the tower is the *High Roller*. Tearing round the outside of the Stratosphere, taking sharp 32-degree turns at a height of 277m (908ft), this is the world's highest rollercoaster.

The name *Insanity – The Ride* speaks for itself. If you are brave enough to attempt it, a 20-m (64-ft) arm protrudes over the edge of the tower where it spins passengers facing downwards at an angle of 90 degrees, experiencing a force of three Gs. At the dizzy height of 274m (900ft), this is the most terrifying way to get an unobstructed view of Las Vegas.

X Scream pushes brave riders to the edge, quite literally. The ride features an open vehicle that propels eight passengers 8.2m (27ft) over the rim of the tower. Riders experience a brief sense of weightlessness as they race towards the ground from a height of 264m (866ft), before the ride drags them back to start all over again.

Speed: The Ride at the Sahara

Rollercoasters on the Strip include the *Manhattan Express* at New York–New York, which races around the hotel skyscrapers reaching heights of 60m (200ft) and speeds of up to 107kph (67mph). The world's largest indoor rollercoaster, the *Canyon Blaster*, double-loops and corkscrews with speeds of up to 88kph (55mph) inside the Circus Circus Adventuredome, while *Speed: the Ride* at the Sahara rockets from 56–112kph (35–70mph), flying through

Entrance to the *Manhattan Express*

underground tunnels and loops before stopping around 69m (225ft) above the ground.

Thirty minutes outside Las Vegas at Buffalo Bills in Primm, visitors can ride the *Adventure Canyon Log Flume* or the famed *Desperado*. With its 69-m (225-ft)

drop, it is one of the largest and tallest rollercoasters in the world.

Finally, for the ultimate extremes in height and speed, you could always try skydiving. Racing towards the earth from a distance of thousands of feet would give you the optimum view of the Strip, Las Vegas, and even four American states. *Skydive Las Vegas* operates outside Las Vegas in Boulder City, otherwise you can try the sport of body flight at *Flyaway Indoor Skydiving* and simulate the freefall experienced in skydiving within a vertical column of air which reaches speeds of up to 192kph (120mph).

See pp142–5 for more information on thrill rides.

The *Manhattan Express* races around New York–New York at over 100kph (63mph)

Hollywood moguls have always been attracted to Las Vegas. As well as investing in property, Tinsel Town big shots have used the city as a luminous backdrop for many classic movies including Jane Russell and Victor Mature in *The Las Vegas Story*, Elvis Presley in *Viva Las Vegas* and Johnny Depp in the dark tale *Fear and Loathing in Las Vegas*.

'In any other town, they'd be the bad guys'

The classic casino heist *Ocean's Eleven* has been filmed twice in Las Vegas. The original movie was made in 1960, starring Frank Sinatra as World War II veteran Danny Ocean who teams up with his ex-army buddies to rob the five

major casinos in Las Vegas, then the Sands, Desert Inn, Flamingo, Sahara and Riviera. In 2001 the movie was remade with George Clooney in the starring role, and on this occasion the gang rob the Bellagio, the Mirage and the MGM Grand. The remake also starred Brad Pitt, Elliott Gould, Matt Damon and Julia Roberts. Although the sequel, *Ocean's Twelve* was set in Europe, it also featured scenes in Las Vegas. To watch both movies provides a glimpse of how the city has evolved over 40 years.

Diamonds Are Forever

Investigating a worldwide smuggling operation, James Bond visits Las Vegas to uncover casino owner Ernst Stavro

Blofeld. Released in 1971 with Sean Connery as 007, *Diamonds Are Forever* was filmed on location in Circus Circus, the Las Vegas Hilton and the Tropicana.

Honeymoon in Vegas

Starring Nicholas Cage, James Caan and Sarah Jessica Parker. Cage plays the hapless Jack Singer who is unable to repay a huge debt after losing a poker game to Tommy Corman (James Caan). Although Jack is in Las Vegas to marry his girlfriend, the only way that he can settle his loss is to allow Corman to spend the weekend with his fiancée Betsy. This hilarious movie was filmed on the Strip in Bally's and also features 34 flying Elvises.

Casino

'No one stays at the top forever' was the tagline of this 1995 movie, which dramatised real-life events that took place at the Stardust Hotel, with the mob's inside man Frank 'Lefty' Rosenthal, his wife Geri and the hot-tempered enforcer Tony 'The Ant' Spilotro. These three roles were played by Robert De Niro, Sharon Stone and Joe Pesci, directed by Martin Scorsese on location at the Jockey Club, the Riviera and the since demolished Landmark.

Vegas Vacation

Starring Chevy Chase as the half-witted Clark Wilhelm Griswold Jr, the family head off to Las Vegas. Their clownish adventures take them to the MGM Grand, the Riviera and the Mirage, where Clark has a close encounter with Siegfried and Roy's white tigers, his wife falls under the charm of Wayne Newton and the Griswolds almost destroy the Hoover Dam.

Las Vegas makes frequent television appearances and has been seen in *The X Files*, *The A Team*, *The Partridge Family*, *The Ed Sullivan Show* and *Perry Mason*. Recent appearances include the hit series *CSI: Crime Scene Investigation* and *Las Vegas* starring James Caan.

Opposite: A boxing match at the MGM Grand provided a distraction from the casino heist in *Ocean's Eleven*
Below: The Stardust, real-life location of the events depicted in *Casino*

The Shark Reef

This one-of-a-kind aquatic experience, the Shark Reef at Mandalay Bay, is home to many exotic and dangerous species. Suitable for all the family, visitors receive a passport-style guide with fun facts, maps and guidelines, as well as a hand-held audio device that explains all of the animals and fish on display.

A majestic stingray

Golden crocodiles
As you enter the Shark Reef, you encounter the golden crocodiles. A hybrid of Siamese and saltwater crocodiles, these are the only examples of this reptile outside Thailand. They may seem harmless as they float sedately on the top of the water, but these are ferocious predators and it would take four men to restrain each one.

Freshwater pool
Next to the crocodiles is a freshwater pool which includes clown loach, bala sharks, the glittering tinfoil barb and the large pink gourami fish, which has a very unusual respiratory system allowing it to breathe air.

Predators
Fearsome hunters and extremely fast runners, water monitors are slightly smaller than their cousin, the Komodo dragon. On display close to these reptiles are several Amazon predators such as the moroto stingray or black pacu and a tank full of piranhas. A shoal of these famously aggressive predators could consume the flesh of an entire cow in minutes.

Reef tunnels
The aquarium features two glass walkthroughs, the Front Reef Tunnel and Back Reef Tunnel, which contain coral reefs populated with vibrant fish such as the stars and stripes puffer, the purple tang or Picasso trigger. Dominating these tunnels, majestic sharks soar over your head and around the tanks at great speed, including the zebra, bonnethead and the black tip reef shark.

Touch pool
Nobody can resist the touch pool. Under the watchful eye of an attraction guide, you can reach into the water and touch friendly stingrays, horseshoe crabs or small sharks.

Jellyfish
To the side of the touch pool is a ghostly display of jellyfish. These creatures are made up of 96 per cent water and drift along the ocean currents feeding on zooplankton. The lighting in their tank gives each creature an eerie glow as they rise then descend gracefully in the darkened tank. Beautiful as they appear, jellyfish can deliver a painful sting and

one touch from the Australian box jellyfish can prove fatal.

Sunken ship

The most impressive display of sea life can be seen around the sunken pirate ship, which is populated by more than 40 different sharks. Housed in 5 million litres (just over 1 million gallons) of water, these predators are joined by sea turtles, moray eels, stingrays and several other species of fish. Sharks in this tank include the lemon shark, one of the most dangerous sharks in the world, and the fearsome-looking sand tiger shark. *The Shark Reef, Mandalay Bay Resort & Casino, 3950 Las Vegas Blvd S. Tel: (702) 632 7580. Open: daily 10am–11pm (last admission 10pm). The attraction is moderately priced with discounts for children and senior citizens. Children under four can visit free.*

Get up close inside one of the reef tunnels

Caesars Palace

Caesars Palace is synonymous with Las Vegas. Across the globe, many aspiring nightclubs, penny arcades and casinos have used its famous name in an effort to give their business the excitement and glamour of Las Vegas, but the original Caesars Palace reigns supreme.

Caesars Palace Fountain Show

Its imperial presence has dominated the landscape since 1966, when the luxury resort based on ancient Rome became the first themed hotel on the Strip. In its 40 years, Caesars Palace has become known for its opulence, with standard guest rooms that include armoires, European-style bathrooms, chaises longues and platform beds, while the suites include private dining rooms, wet bars, in-room saunas and steam rooms.

Since Andy Williams opened the Circus Maximus showroom in Caesars in 1966, the Palace has played host to an impressive list of headliners and to many star-studded television shows and specials, and now the newly completed Colosseum presents shows starring Céline Dion and Elton John.

The main entrance to Caesars Palace is set back a little from the Strip. You can walk through the gardens, ornamented with Roman statues and fountains, or use the moving walkways each side of the property. As in every Las Vegas hotel, from the main entrance you walk right into the casino. One difference with Caesars Palace is that the casino entrance is not surrounded by rows of slot machines, but you will see table games when you reach the interior. Card dealers and croupiers dress in black and gold, cocktail waitresses in toga-inspired costumes fuss around the clientele, while the slot machines are located to the right of the property in a second casino area.

Between these two casinos there is a selection of restaurants and bars including the Hyakumi Japanese Restaurant and Sushi Bar along with Cleopatra's Barge, an ornate floating cocktail bar.

For fine dining, restaurants include Hawaiian cuisine at 8-0-8, Bradley Ogden, Wolfgang Puck's celebrated Spago and Chinois, the new restaurant Guy Savoy, Empress Court, Neros, The Palm and Italian cuisine at Terrazza. Casual diners can enjoy Bertolini's, Café Lago, Cheesecake Factory, Cypress Market, La Salsa, Stage Deli and Planet Hollywood.

Caesars Palace is also famed for its Forum Shops – over 65,000sq m (700,000sq ft) of retail space in a beautiful shopping centre featuring Roman architecture set beneath an ever-changing

All hotels are air conditioned, but can prove quite chilly if you are not used to it. Take an extra layer of clothing if you will be sitting still in a bar or restaurant for a few hours.

deep-blue sky. Children will love the tropical fish tanks and the talking statues, although these displays are equally captivating for the adults if they can resist the lure of stores such as Louis Vuitton, Escada, Gucci, Guess, Christian Dior, Nike Town, Virgin Records Megastore, Fendi, Polo/Ralph Lauren and Hugo Boss.

After dark, Caesars Palace has a vibrant nightlife with bars and clubs that include the celebrated Asian-themed OPM, liberal servings at the Galleria Bar, erotic silhouette dancers at the Shadow Bar, musical performance at the Terrazza Lounge and the captivating Sea Horse Lounge.

The vast Caesars Palace complex

Tour: Virtual history

While Las Vegas offers cuisine, culture and entertainment from around the world, you can also travel through the centuries. At the Las Vegas Hilton, you can see into the future with *Star Trek: the Experience*, while the Strip transports you back in time to medieval England, ancient Rome and Egypt.

Allow one day. Use the monorails to reach resorts.

1 The Victorian Room
Start your day with breakfast at the Victorian Room at Barbary Coast. Located at the back of the casino, close to the Flamingo Road entrance, this themed restaurant also specialises in Chinese food, but offers a great-value breakfast menu. This small restaurant is very popular so expect to queue if you arrive after 8am.
Located between Bally's and The Flamingo. Open: 24 hours.
Head west along Flamingo Road, past the junction with the Strip.

2 Caesars Palace
Head across the Strip to the magnificent

A giant sphinx guards the entrance to Luxor

Caesars Palace. Mob aficionados once likened this resort to historic Sicily rather than ancient Rome, but the resort has undergone many changes in nearly 40 years. In 1967 Evel Knievel attempted to jump the resort's fountains (then the largest in the world) by motorbike, which proved to be a near-fatal stunt.
See also pp52–3.

3 The Forum Shops
Roman streetscapes under a changeable blue sky. Several Strip resorts have adopted this interior concept, but Caesars will always be credited as the first. *Shoppus til you Droppus* is their motto, and you can watch statues of Venus, Apollo and Bacchus come to life in an atmospheric display of rain, fire and mist under a thunderstruck sky. The Forum Shops are also home to a 190,000 litre (50,190 gallon) aquarium and you can take a virtual-reality thrill ride through time with *Race for Atlantis*.
Open: daily 10am–11pm (weekends until midnight). The Fountain Shows run every hour on the hour.
Retrace your steps along Flamingo Road and turn right down the Strip. Keep going south until you are past Reno Avenue.

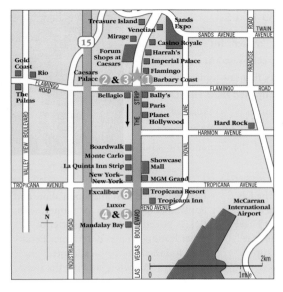

1922 discovery, every item has been reproduced using ancient Egyptian-style techniques and positioned where they were originally discovered.
Open: daily 9am–11pm.
Head north on the Strip and stop just before Tropicana Avenue.

6 Tournament of the Kings

End your day with a good old-fashioned English joust at the Excalibur. Its design is similar to the fairytale castle Neuschwanstein built between 1869 and 1886 for the eccentric King Ludwig II of Bavaria, which also inspired Sleeping Beauty's castle at Disneyland. Beyond the portcullis and courtyards you can tuck into a messy medieval feast at the *Tournament of The Kings* dinner show where knives and forks are off the menu and you can scream and holler at a cast of over 100 performers as they lock swords and fight dragons in King Arthur's Arena.
Shows daily at 6pm and 8.30pm. Book early to avoid disappointment.

4 The Luxor

When the Luxor first opened in 1993, its stunning architecture was unlike any other building to appear on the Strip. By night the pyramid emits the world's brightest beam from its tip, a 40-billion candlepower projection which can be seen by pilots in Los Angeles. The entrance to the pyramid is protected by a giant sphinx, while the interior houses an open-plan design reflecting Luxor and Karnak, all finished with hieroglyphics. While in the hotel, visit the Pharoah's Pavilion at the gateway to the world's largest atrium.

5 The Tomb and Museum of King Tutankhamun

The only authentic replica of the tomb of King Tutankhamun outside of Egypt. Laid out according to Howard Carter's

The Excalibur

Girls! Girls! Girls!

Las Vegas has always been known for its beautiful showgirls, and has become the celebrated home to several erotic revues. Theatre audiences first saw topless showgirls in 1957 when Minsky's Follies opened their *Holiday for G Strings* production at the Dunes – a cause of great controversy, but a huge commercial success that ran for over four years and kick-started the demand for adult entertainment in Las Vegas.

City of showgirls

The longest-running show on the Las Vegas Strip is Tropicana's *Folies Bergère*. Appearing in the hotel's Tiffany Theater twice nightly, the show presents first-rate variety acts with the city's top showgirls, although the earlier performance features fully clothed dancers. As well as new production numbers, the show also showcases the best of previous *Folies*.

Another long-established Las Vegas production is *Bottoms Up* at the Flamingo, the only topless afternoon show. This highly acclaimed production has been voted best afternoon show and applauded for its value for money, with tickets priced at almost a quarter of other leading revues. Entertainer Breck Wall founded this musical comedy in Dallas in 1959 before moving the show to Las Vegas five years later. With its Vaudevillian theme, delivering old-fashioned laughs, the cast includes several comic regulars with male and female dancers.

Direct from the Crazy Horse in Paris, where it has been an attraction since 1951, *La Femme* is described as an adults-only exploration of sensuality. Appearing at the La Femme Theater at the MGM Grand, 12 ballet-trained members from the original Crazy Horse production open the show in British military uniform singing 'God save our bare skins' to

The Riviera: home to the revue *Splash*

Folies Bergère at the Tropicana

the tune of the English national anthem, before the show goes on to use film projections and lighting effects to bathe the dancers' bodies in a multitude of colours and patterns. Most topless shows are for over-18s only but audience members must be over 21 to see this show, where the dress code is described as business-casual.

Another famed Vegas production is *Splash* at the Riviera, a dynamic variety performance with tribute artists, motorcycle daredevils, topless showgirls and dance numbers ranging from classical routines to high-energy street and jazz. Figure and adagio ice skaters perform on a custom-designed skating rink, within a show that also includes Argentinian entertainers and the Los Latin Cowboys who interact with the audience, along with the hilarious juggling routines performed by the Richard Brothers.

On the same theme, other Las Vegas revues include *Fantasy* at the Luxor, the rock 'n' roll themed *Erocktica* at the Rio and topless vampires in *Bite* at the Stratosphere.

Finally, in true Sin City style, Las Vegas recently opened the first Hooters Hotel and Casino on Tropicana Avenue. Famed for its singing, hula-hooping, all-American hooters girls, the company has created over 375 beach-themed restaurants in 46 counties, and has even started its own airline.

And for the ladies, Las Vegas delivers the *Chippendales* at the Rio, *Men of Russia* at the Suncoast and Australia's *Thunder Down Under* at the Excalibur.

The best views of the Strip

There are several good vantage points to see the best view of Las Vegas Boulevard, or the Strip as it is known today. Day or night, try to catch an aerial view of the city, available from several high-rise locations.

View from the Eiffel Tower

The Stratosphere Tower

At the northern tip of the Las Vegas Strip, the Stratosphere Tower stands at a lofty 345m (1,132ft). The tallest free-standing observation tower in the USA, it is visible from most areas in Las Vegas, and when you see the city skyline from a distance the Stratosphere stands as a marker, with the Strip extending southward and Downtown Las Vegas clustered beyond it to the north.

At the top of the Stratosphere, the observation deck provides breathtaking views, a lounge to relax in, and fine dining at The Top of the World, a high-rise restaurant that rotates 360 degrees for the optimum views of Las Vegas.

The Stratosphere is well known for its thrill rides (*see pp46–7*). If the tower isn't tall enough, the *Big Shot* fires riders upwards to the very tip of the needle, the *High Roller* rollercoaster hurtles around the top of the building, *X Scream* propels eight terrified riders headfirst over the tower edge, while *Insanity – the Ride* spins its passengers face down over Las Vegas.
Open: daily 10am–1am (Fri & Sat until 2am). Admission fee: inexpensive, discounted for children and senior citizens. The admission fee is higher if you include the thrill rides.

The *Eiffel Tower Experience*

In the heart of the Strip stands Paris Las Vegas. Beyond its stunning architecture, the interior features cobbled walkways and Parisian streetscapes under a deep-blue sky. Paris was opened in 1999, with 32-storey guest towers that offer magnificent Strip views, if your room is ideally located,

Night-time helicopter tours provide a stunning view of Las Vegas

maybe including the *Fountains at Bellagio* across the Boulevard.

The hotel is famed for its replicas of the Arc de Triomphe and the Eiffel Tower, which is an exact reproduction of its Parisian forefather. Visitors can buy admission to the *Eiffel Tower Experience*, which transports you 138m (453ft) upwards to a panoramic view of Las Vegas from the centre of the Strip. *Open: 10am–1am. Moderately priced, discounted for children and senior citizens. Prices higher Fri & Sat. Tickets are available in the tower box office on the Strip and in hotel gift shops.*

Mon Ami Gabi
Not a high-rise view, but for fine dining alfresco, Mon Ami Gabi offers French cuisine in the warmth of the desert sun. Located at Paris in the middle of the Strip, you can sit outside and watch the world rush by on the Las Vegas Strip, and by night you have the ideal view of the Bellagio fountains.

Strip tours by helicopter
The greatest aerial view of Las Vegas is from a helicopter. Many tour companies offer helicopter trips to the Grand Canyon or the Hoover Dam, and nightly tours of the Las Vegas Strip.
Las Vegas Helicopters, 3712 Las Vegas Blvd S (next to Bellagio).
Tel: (702) 736 0013/(888) 779 0800.
www.lvhelicopters.com

The *Eiffel Tower Experience* offers a panoramic view of the Strip

Bellagio

The magnificent Bellagio hotel is the essence of Las Vegas opulence and style. Based on the northern Italian village of the same name, its grand opening took place in October 1998. At the base of the resort, surrounding the lake, is a collection of bars and restaurants, designed to recreate village properties found around the hotel's namesake on Lake Como.

Display in the conservatory

There are moving walkways, and side entrances from Caesars Palace and through the Via Bellagio shops. Once inside the hotel, its $1.6-billion price tag is more than evident. One stunning feature is the ceiling of the hotel lobby, the Fiore di Como, with over 2,000 suspended glass flowers, each one unique, before you cast your eyes downwards to the breathtaking marble walkways which guide you through the casino and out towards the Bellagio Conservatory and Botanical Gardens, presenting an impressive display of flora in keeping with the current season or major holidays.

In the same area you will often see a queue forming for the popular Buffet at Bellagio, and you will be impressed by the sweeping staircases leading towards the spa and wedding chapels.

Bellagio has many casual and fine-dining restaurants throughout the property, although some of its lakeside establishments may not be within everyone's price range. Hotel restaurants include the 24-hour Café Bellagio, Nectar, Café Gelato and the Buffet at Bellagio, or you can sample award-winning pastries at Jean-Phillipe Patisserie or take high tea at the Petrossian Bar. The resort offers a world of cuisine with Italian food at Circo, Chinese at Jasmine, Japanese food at Shintaro, French dining at the award-

THE FOUNTAINS AT BELLAGIO

One of the most spectacular free shows on the Las Vegas Strip is the choreographed display *Fountains at Bellagio*. Dancing streams of water are created by water-emitting devices, named oarsmen, in addition to mini-shooters and super-shooters that can reach a height of 72m (240ft). Over 1,000 fountains span more than 300m (1,000ft) across Lake Bellagio to create the largest musical fountain system in the world. The displays are choreographed to music ranging from Luciano Pavarotti and Andrea Bocelli to Gene Kelly, Frank Sinatra and Lionel Ritchie. The display can be seen from both sides of the Strip, but if the sidewalk is too crowded with onlookers, the bridge that connects Bellagio with Bally's offers a good vantage point.

Free shows 3pm–midnight (Sat & Sun midday–midnight). Every 30 minutes until 8pm, then every 15 minutes.

The Bellagio Conservatory and Botanical Gardens

winning Le Cirque and Picasso, and lake-side dining at Todd English's Olives.

Bellagio is home to the Cirque du Soleil's acclaimed production 'O', with a cast of 81 artists performing in, on and above a 5.7-million-litre (1.2-million-gallon) pool of water.

The Bellagio is also famed for its gallery of fine art, home to many prestigious international collections. *See p76. You must be at least 18 years of age to enter the Bellagio unless you are staying there.*

Fountains at Bellagio, the largest water fountain system in the world

Tour: After dark

Known as a 24-hour city, Las Vegas really comes to life after dark. Wander through a casino at any hour, even 4am, and you will see riotous dice games and weary gamblers still trying to even up their percentages on the blackjack tables. Some of the Strip's greatest attractions are offered during the twilight hours and the city is famed for its huge variety of nightlife and entertainment.

Allow one evening.

1 Monte Carlo

Start your evening in the French Riviera and the Monte Carlo resort. Inspired by the Place du Casino in Monte Carlo, the whole resort is one tenth of the size of Monaco and offers European roulette tables, which have only one zero on the wheel compared to American wheels with the zero and double-zero options. Any adept gambler will explain that this slightly increases the player's percentage against the casino. The Monte Carlo is home to acclaimed gourmet restaurants such as Andre's, with its mouthwatering French cuisine and decor, along with Blackstone's for the very best in all-American beef. Watch chefs prepare your chosen dishes at The Buffet at Monte Carlo, acclaimed as one of the best on the Strip, or sample home beers at the Monte Carlo Pub & Brewery, which also offers a great menu.

Map labels:

DESERT INN ROAD
SPRING MOUNTAIN ROAD
VALLEY VIEW BOULEVARD
INDUSTRIAL ROAD
THE STRIP
CONVENTION CENTER
Stardust
Elvis-A-Rama
New Frontier
DESERT INN ROAD
Fashion Show Mall
Wynn Las Vegas
Treasure Island 5
Sands Expo
Venetian 4
Mirage
SANDS AVENUE
Casino Royale
Forum Shops at Caesars
Harrah's
Imperial Palace
Gold Coast
Rio
Flamingo
Caesars Palace
Barbary Coast
FLAMINGO ROAD
The Palms 6
Bellagio 2
Bally's
Paris 3
Planet Hollywood
HARMON AVENUE
KOVAL LANE
Boardwalk
Monte Carlo 1
Showcase Mall
La Quinta Inn Strip
The Orleans
New York–New York
MGM Grand
TROPICANA AVENUE
Excalibur
Hooters
Tropicana Resort
Tropicana Inn
RENO AVENUE
Luxor
Mandalay Bay
LAS VEGAS BLVD
McCarran International Airport
0 1km
0 1mile

Go north along the Strip until just before the junction with Flamingo Road.

2 The Fountains at Bellagio
This wonderful display starts at 3pm, but is far more impressive by night.
See pp60–61.
Go across the street.

3 The *Eiffel Tower Experience*
Even if you have seen this attraction by day, by night Las Vegas is a whole new city. Travel 100 storeys above the city to the top of this Parisian landmark and see Las Vegas in all its neon glory.
Open: daily 10am–1am. Head north on the Strip, past the Forum Shops.

4 The Mirage Volcano
Every evening the peaceful waterfalls outside this Polynesian-themed resort transform into a volcanic eruption with fiery red lights, gas jets and explosions that reach 30m (100ft). This is a very popular attraction, so find your place early, preferably at the end of the previous eruption.
Free shows every 15 minutes, 8pm–midnight.
Go a little further north on the Strip.

5 *The Sirens of TI*
Set on an impressive 17th-century set, *The Sirens of TI* features high-diving acrobatics and daring swordplay. As the seductive Sirens mesmerise the captain and crew of The Bull, the superstitious pirates soon doubt the good intentions of these temptresses and a riotous battle ensues. The show is suitable for family viewing, with a VIP viewing area for hotel guests.
Show times: 5.30pm, 7.00pm, 8.30pm and 10.00pm in Sirens' Cove at the front entrance of TI – Treasure Island Hotel and Casino.

6 Ghostbar at Palms
Grab a taxi and head to the Palms resort on West Flamingo Road where the Ghostbar on the 55th floor offers 3.6m (12ft) floor-to-ceiling windows and the sky deck features a 360° view of the Strip. This is a popular bar, so get there early if you do not want to queue.
Open: daily 8pm–early morning.

The Mirage Volcano erupts every 15 minutes

Las Vegas magic

Magic shows are big business in Las Vegas. Signs advertising hotel attractions flicker with images of illusionists and big-budget stunts from some of the greatest names in sorcery.

Billboard at the Monte Carlo

One legendary Las Vegas duo, recognised globally as a symbol for the city, are **Siegfried and Roy**. Featuring royal white tigers and rare breeds of wild cats, Siegfried and Roy's celebrated stage show ran at the Mirage for thirteen years with 5,750 sold-out performances and earned them the title of Magicians of the Century. The show reached a sudden end in October 2003, when illusionist Roy Horn was attacked on stage by his white tiger Montecore. Although the show has ended, they continue to preserve the rare cats in their care, and have dedicated a 32-hectare (80-acre) estate to their animals, along with *The Secret Garden of Siegfried & Roy* at the Mirage (*see p136*).

Renegade magicians Penn and Teller are in residence at the Rio. Working together for over 25 years, they describe themselves as 'a couple of eccentric guys who have learned to do a few cool things.'

They are award-winning stars of television and Broadway, best-selling authors and several times winners of the Las Vegas Magicians of the Year. Their show features escape acts, stunts with knives, showgirls and even a gorilla, before the two friends shoot each other with .357 Magnums and catch the bullets in their teeth.

The hottest magician on the Strip is Lance Burton, who resides at the Monte Carlo, in the plush $27-million Lance Burton Theatre. An expert in his craft, his breathtaking family show often enlists the help of audience members, as he makes objects appear, disappear or

Lance Burton: Master Magician

levitate before the audience and even makes a car vanish into space.

A little further up the Strip is Rick Thomas at the Stardust. His highly acclaimed show features his beloved tigers Kyra, Maximillian, Rocky, Zeus and Samson – a 215-kg (475-lb) Royal White Bengal Tiger. Then, if you are ever curious to see how a live goldfish can appear over an audience member's head, visit Mac King's act at Harrah's, including visual comedy, sleight of hand and great entertainment for one of the most competitive prices on the Strip.

When he's not walking through the Great Wall of China or making the Statue of Liberty disappear, David Copperfield appears as a headliner in Las Vegas. Acclaimed as the Greatest Illusionist of all our Time, his recent engagements have included the MGM Grand.

TOP SHOWS

Penn and Teller appear daily (except Tuesday). Tickets are moderately priced, although the show is not suitable for children.
Rio All-Suite Hotel & Casino, 3700 W. Flamingo Rd. Tel: (702) 777 7776.
Lance Burton performs Tuesday to Saturday. Tickets are moderately priced for this high-quality family entertainment.
Lance Burton Theatre, Monte Carlo Resort & Casino, 3770 Las Vegas Blvd. South. Tel: (702) 730 7160.
The Magic of Rick Thomas can be seen Thursday to Tuesday at the Stardust and tickets are inexpensive.
Stardust Resort & Casino, 3000 Las Vegas Blvd. South. Tel: (702) 732 6325.
See your hotel box office or magazine listings for all current shows.

Penn and Teller at the Rio: 'If you're lucky, no one gets hurt.'

Tour: Las Vegas fantasy

In 1989, visionary Steve Wynn started a new era of resort building when the Mirage opened on the Strip. A wave of themed successors quickly followed in the shape of the Excalibur, Luxor, MGM Grand and Treasure Island. It changed the course of history for Las Vegas, offering resorts that didn't just cater for gamblers but created a fantasy world for all the family.

Allow one day. Use the Las Vegas monorail to reach some resorts.

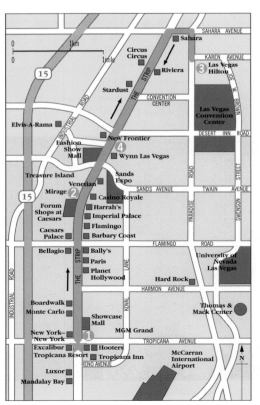

1 MGM Grand

With 5,000 rooms, this creation of MGM magnate Kirk Kerkorian was the largest hotel in the world when it opened, costing a million dollars for each day of construction. Still one of the largest hotels in the world, this Hollywood-themed resort is spacious and easy to negotiate for visitors, with pictures of Hollywood starlets and leading men gracing the walls. The ceiling above the main casino is decorated with a Tinsel Town mural and even the MGM trademark lion is honoured with the MGM Grand Lion Habitat (*see p136*). *Head north along the Strip to the Mirage.*

2 The Mirage

At a cost of $630 million, Steve Wynn opened the Mirage in 1989, a resort he stated would bring people to Las Vegas in the same way that Disneyland attracted visitors to Orlando. Fronted by a 1.2-hectare (3-acre) lagoon and volcano, the resort's palm-tree-lined drive leads visitors into a South Seas paradise, with a tropical atrium, over 27m (90ft) high, with waterfalls, exotic palms, orchids and flora, which dwell aside bubbling lagoons and a 91-litre (20,000-gallon) aquarium containing over 90 species of tropical fish. The Mirage is also home to *Siegfried and Roy's Secret Garden* and *Dolphin Habitat*, as well as their beloved *White Tiger Habitat.*

Stop for a meal at the highly acclaimed *Cravings – The Ultimate Buffet Experience*, designed to resemble an international bazaar by Adam Tihany, designer of *Le Cirque 2000* in New York.

The MGM Grand Lion Habitat

Lunch is served Monday–Friday 11am–3pm, or their Champagne Brunch is served weekends from 8am. Dinner is served from 3pm–10pm.
Continue north along the Strip, then turn right on Sahara Ave and head south towards the Las Vegas Hilton, straight ahead on Paradise Road.

3 *Star Trek: The Experience*
Head over to the Las Vegas Hilton and lose yourself in the 24th century. Battle against the enemy in *Klingon Encounter* or take a chance against terrifying drones in *Borg Invasion 4D.*
Star Trek: The Experience is open Sun–Thur, 11am–10pm. Fri and Sat until 11pm.
Head back to the Strip, then south to Wynn.

4 *Le Rêve: A Small Collection of Imperfect Dreams*
Book tickets for this incredible show created by Steve Wynn and the award-winning Franco Dragone. Described as visually stunning and featuring artists and athletes from around the globe, the theatre's unique round design allows every audience member to be centre stage.
Shows Sat–Wed 7.30pm and 10.30pm.
Wynn Las Vegas, 3131 S. Las Vegas Blvd. Tel: (702) 770 7000.

It would take nearly 14 years to spend a night in each bed at the MGM Grand, and if you stacked each bed in a pile you could create a tower over ten times as high as the Empire State Building.

The final frontier

From a 21st-century city, take a visit just off the Las Vegas Strip to a 24th-century frontier in *Star Trek: The Experience*. Located at the Las Vegas Hilton on Paradise Road, this multi-million dollar attraction is one experience not to miss.

The Las Vegas Hilton

The first episode of *Star Trek* was aired on 8 September 1966 and became the most successful show in television syndicate history. It spawned merchandise, movies, magazines and further television incarnations such as *Star Trek: the Next Generation, Deep Space Nine, Voyager* and *Enterprise*.

Star Trek conventions in the United States attract over 300,000 visitors every year, but it is here at the Las Vegas Hilton that not only Trekkies, but any visitor, can experience one of the most enjoyable and fascinating attractions in the whole city.

Encounter and *Borg Invasion 4D*. Battle against fierce warriors in *Klingon Encounter* as you travel at warp speed in a shuttlecraft and invade a Klingon warship, then prepare to be assimilated in *Borg Invasion 4D*. Featuring live actors and special effects, with 23,000 watts of 12-channel sound and 3D film effects, the drones try to capture guests to join their collective. To see how these rides and special effects are created visit *Star Trek: The Experience – Secrets Revealed*, for a revealing behind-the-scenes look at the technology behind these attractions.

History of the Future Museum

With displays of props, spacecraft, costumes, masks and weaponry, this museum charts the history of the USS *Enterprise* and her crew, along with other Star Fleet vessels, personnel and enemies.

Klingon Encounter and *Borg Invasion 4D*

Star Trek: The Experience is home to two exciting new rides, *Klingon*

Entrance to *Star Trek: The Experience*

Voyager and the *Enterprise*, the pride of Starfleet

Deep Space Nine Promenade

The retail outlets in *Star Trek: The Experience* boast the largest selection of Star Trek merchandise in the universe. Here you can purchase any items from pens and keyrings to authentic Klingon uniforms costing $12,000. Children's toys, T-shirts, kitchen accessories, jewellery and Star Trek outfits for all crew members are among the vast collections of memorabilia in one of the most compelling gift shops in the city. Licensed merchandise can be found at Zek's Grand Emporium, including a selection of Star Trek souvenirs, videos and DVDs, while the Admiral Collection features authentic Star Trek masks created by award-winning Hollywood make-up artist Michael Westmore, along with props created by Paramount.

The Space Quest Casino accompanies the attraction, while refreshments are served in Quark's Bar & Restaurant. Quark also has his own line of merchandise available at Moogie's Trading Post. Then, to prove to your friends that you really did visit the final frontier, you can have your image superimposed onto a series of Star Trek scenarios, where you can sit on the bridge and captain the *Enterprise.*

STAR TREK: THE EXPERIENCE

You can buy all-day passes to the museum and ride, or pay a reduced price for the museum only. Reductions are available for senior citizens and children. You do not need a ticket to visit the retail areas, Quark's Bar & Restaurant or the Space Quest Casino. *Las Vegas Hilton, 3000 Paradise Road. Tel: (702) 732 5111. Open: daily 11am–10pm (Sat 11pm).*

Luminous, iconic and sparkling with jewels, Elvis Presley is a true mascot for Las Vegas.

His reign started in the late 1960s. After appearing in a succession of Hollywood movies, and eight years after his last concert appearance, Elvis made his live stage comeback at the International Hotel (now the Las Vegas Hilton).

Opening on 31 July 1969, Elvis was booked for a four-week 57-show engagement that broke every box office record in the city. Following his triumphant opening performance, Elvis's enterprising manager, Colonel Tom Parker, hastily negotiated a contract with hotel executive Alex Shoofey, which they scribbled across a drink-stained hotel tablecloth and honoured until 1976, when Elvis gave his final performance in the city.

Elvis Presley had skyrocketed to fame in 1956, with his debut single *Heartbreak Hotel*. As his records became million-sellers, and Hollywood

Work or play, Elvis was a frequent visitor to Las Vegas. In 1964 he filmed *Viva Las Vegas* in the city. The movie used locations such as the Flamingo and the Sahara, then closed with a wedding scene set in the Little Church of the West, which is now located south of the Las Vegas Strip. Three years later, Elvis returned for the real thing when he broke teenage hearts by marrying Priscilla Beaulieu at the Aladdin Hotel in May 1967.

beckoned, it seemed fitting that Elvis should appear in Las Vegas, and on 23 April 1956 he made his debut appearance at the New Frontier Hotel.

Compared to his later performances in the 1970s, Elvis's initial engagement did little to impress his Las Vegas audience. Previously known as the Last Frontier, the hotel had recently been remodelled into a space-age resort where Elvis appeared in the futuristic new showroom as 'The Atomic Powered Singer'. However, without his usual teenage audience, Elvis did little to distract the gamblers from the lure of the gaming tables.

Thirteen years later, when he stepped back into the spotlight at the International, Elvis conquered Las Vegas. He was booked for two lengthy engagements each year, and he sold out two shows every evening for weeks on end.

No other artist can boast the impact that Elvis had on Las Vegas, and it is still evident today. Whether rocking the lounge bars or headlining the Strip, Elvis is everywhere. Proof indeed that over a quarter of a century after his death, Elvis never truly left the building.

Opposite: One of many Elvis impersonators in Las Vegas
Below: The Frontier, where Elvis made his first Vegas appearance

Across the globe, Elvis impersonators far outnumber any other tribute artists. In Las Vegas alone, Elvis can command your wedding services or serve you cocktails, and he even has his own professional skydiving team known as the *Flying Elvises*.

Tour: The Elvis tour

You cannot avoid Elvis in Las Vegas. The singer spent many years working in the city, and devoted fans can spend days locating every Elvis sight. Although there have been dramatic changes since Elvis's day, there are still many fascinating landmarks, museums and shows relating to the King of Vegas.

Allow one day. Use the Las Vegas monorail to reach some resorts.

1 The Las Vegas Hilton
Originally known as the International, Elvis made his stage comeback in the hotel showroom on 31 July 1969. As you enter the Hilton, a bronze statue commemorating Elvis's sold-out performances is to your right in front of the casino. The showroom, which was once the largest in the city, still exists and is located behind the casino on the ground floor. Its entrance is in the far right-hand corner, but you will be unable to gain access without a show ticket.

Head west on Convention Center to the Strip, then south to the New Frontier.

2 The Frontier Hotel
On 23 April, 1956 Elvis made his Las Vegas debut in the Venus Room at the New Frontier Hotel but his engagement bombed. 'He was very popular with the

His influence is everywhere…

Other Elvis sights in the city include his 1976 El Dorado in the Auto Collection at the Imperial Palace, and the Flamingo and Sahara hotels where Elvis filmed scenes from his movie *Viva Las Vegas*.

At the time of writing, the singer's estate is developing a new attraction in the city, which they claim will give Elvis Presley an even greater presence in Las Vegas.

young girls,' explained publicist Bruce Banke, 'but unfortunately they don't shoot craps.'

Head south along the Strip to the Venetian.

3 Madame Tussaud's

Sing with the King and experience Elvis in concert at the Venetian, where you can place a scarf around Elvis's neck or join him on stage for a photo. This waxwork bears an incredible resemblance to Elvis and, if that doesn't make the hairs on your neck stand on end, he'll even talk to you when touched.

Continue south on the Strip, turning left on Harmon Ave.

4 The Hard Rock Hotel

With a huge neon guitar emblazoned across its entrance, this is a must-see resort for any rock 'n' roll fan. The hotel features a unique memorabilia collection, with Elvis items that include movie costumes, such as his boxing robe from *Kid Galahad* and his customised 1970 Gibson Dove Guitar. Elvis's caped jumpsuit known as the 'Comet' or 'Adonis' is also part of the collection, which he wore during one of his sold-out shows at Madison Square Garden in 1972. The hotel's collection also includes costumes and artefacts belonging to a wide range of performers from Bill Haley and Gene Vincent, to Madonna, Kid Rock and the Rolling Stones. Continuing the Elvis theme, it also includes Geri Halliwell's faux Elvis jumpsuit, worn when she appeared with the Spice Girls at the Billboard Music Awards in 1997.

ELVIS IMPERSONATORS

Las Vegas offers a bounty of impersonators and tribute shows to choose from and you can take your pick from current shows listed in free tourist publications such as *Showbiz*. If he is in town when you visit, do not miss Trent Carlini and his show *The Dream King*. Carlini is a regular in Las Vegas and is famed for his uncanny likeness to Elvis.

The Venetian

With Italian streetscapes, serenading gondoliers and dining in St Mark's Square or alongside the Grand Canal, Las Vegas has captured one of the most romantic cities in Europe with the luxurious Venetian. Located on the Las Vegas Strip close to the junction with Spring Mountain Road and Sands Avenue, the Venetian stands on the former site of the legendary Sands Hotel. With its breathtaking architecture, world-famous museums and entertainment, the Venetian is firmly established as a victorious successor.

The Campanile Tower

The public areas of the Venetian are split into two main levels. Walk in at street level and you will be astounded by the beautiful ceiling artwork and interior design. The casino and hotel lobby are in this area, as well as bars, restaurants and food court including Santa Lucia Café, Cocolini, Rialto Deli, San Gennaro Grill and Pizzaria de Enzo. The Grand Lux Café is situated at the rear of the casino and, with over 150 dishes, it boasts one of the broadest menus in the restaurant industry.

The Guggenheim Hermitage Museum (*see pp76–7*) is also on the casino level. The exhibits change approximately twice a year, and can be seen daily from 9.30am. For celebrity snapshots, keep your camera handy for Madame Tussaud's Celebrity Encounter, where you can have your photograph taken alongside your favourite stars. Located at the front of the Venetian by the Campanile Tower, Madame Tussaud's is open daily from 10am. There is an admission charge for both museums.

GRAND CANAL SHOPPES ENTERTAINMENT

Street performers, opera singers and costumed entertainers perform throughout the Grand Canal Shoppes and feature:

Artisti del Arté – classically trained performers from across the globe who take you back in time to Renaissance Venice in St Mark's Square from 11.30am.

The Venetian Living Statues – performing daily in St Mark's Square and the Oculus lounge on the casino level.

The Gondolier March – from the food court, daily at 9.45am and 4.15pm, gondoliers march through the shopping area to St Mark's Square.

On the second level of the Venetian are the Grand Canal Shoppes, certainly one of the most impressive retail areas in Las Vegas. It can be reached via escalators throughout the casino, or via the Rialto Bridge walkway, located to the right of the Venetian looking from the Strip. With over 46,470sq m (500,000sq ft) of retail space, the shops are set around a reproduction of Venice's Grand Canal, complete with singing gondoliers who serenade visitors under a dusk-blue sky, while the stunning central point of the shopping area is based on St Mark's Square. There are also many coffee shops and restaurants on this level, with a food court that includes Haagen-Dazs, Krispy Kreme, LA Italian Kitchen, Original California Juice Bar, Panda Express, Shake 'n' Burger, Towers Deli and Vico's Burrito.

In keeping with all Las Vegas resorts, the hotel offers an impressive selection of fine dining and night-time entertainment, although visitors can also relax in the *Canyon Ranch Spa Club*. This 6,410sq m (69,000sq ft), two-level health and fitness facility is one of the largest of its kind in North America and is open daily from 5.30am.

The Venetian features stunning replicas of Venice architecture

Tour: City of culture

Las Vegas

THE STRIP

Moulded by the 20th century, Las Vegas has developed its own customs, language, technology, literature and traditions. In a city of make-believe it is hard to imagine that behind the gaming tables, showgirls and all-you-can-eat buffets, Las Vegas is the esteemed home for many priceless works of art.

Allow 5 hours.

There are admission charges for these exhibits.
See pp140–41 for more details.

1 Bellagio Gallery of Fine Art
This elegant resort is a work of art in its own right (*see pp60–61*), but it also houses the Bellagio Gallery of Fine Art, which was opened by developer Steve Wynn in 1998.

The gallery features travelling exhibits from across the globe and recent exhibitions include *The Impressionist*

Breathtaking ceiling artwork at the Venetian

Landscape: From Corot to Van Gogh, featuring 34 masterworks from the European collection at the Museum of Fine Art in Boston. Paintings from 16 world-famous artists such as Monet, Millet, Cézanne and Corot include the vibrant *Forest Interior* by Paul Gauguin, Vincent van Gogh's *Houses at Auvers*, and *Girls Picking Flowers in a Meadow* by Pierre-Auguste Renoir.
Check local guides for the current exhibition. Open: daily 9am–10pm (last entrance 9.30pm). You must be over 18 years old to enter this resort unless you are staying there.
Head north on the Strip.

2 Guggenheim Hermitage Museum
A joint venture between the Hermitage Museum in St Petersburg and the Solomon R Guggenheim Foundation in New York, this museum offers world-class exhibits that change approximately twice a year. Recent displays have included *RUSSIA! The Majesty of the Tsars: Treasures from the Kremlin Museum*, featuring the opulent and most valued possessions of the tsars,

from the collection of the armoury chamber in the Kremlin Museum, Moscow. These priceless 16th- and 17th-century pieces of Russian art form the most comprehensive collection on display since the end of the Cold War. *Check local guides for the current exhibition. The Guggenheim Hermitage is located at the Venetian Hotel. Open: daily 9.30am–8.30pm.*
Continue north, past Sands Avenue.

An exhibition at the Venetian

3 The Wynn Collection

Steve Wynn started his impressive collection in the mid-1990s, which later earned him recognition as one of *ARTnews* magazine's Top Ten Art Collectors in the world. The original name for his new resort, before he renamed it Wynn, was *Le Rêve* or The Dream after Pablo Picasso's famous painting of his mistress, which is proudly displayed in his collection. Although the price Wynn paid for this 1932 masterpiece is unknown, the previous owner paid $44 million for the painting at Christie's in New York. The priceless Wynn collection of 16th- to 20th-century masterworks includes Vermeer's *A Young Woman Seated at the Virginals*, one of only 36 Vermeers known to exist, Rembrandt's *Self-Portrait, Among the Roses* by Pierre-Auguste Renoir, *The Persian Robe* by Henri Matisse and *Steve Wynn (Red, White, Gold)* by Andy Warhol. *Located at Wynn Las Vegas. Open: daily 10am–11pm (Fri & Sat until midnight).*

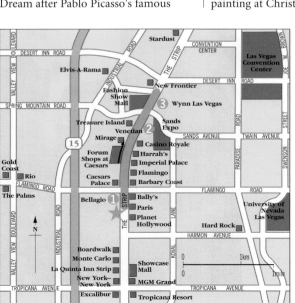

Off The Strip

Away from Las Vegas Boulevard, hotels offer the same glitz and luxury as on the Strip, but the room rates can be extremely competitive. Some of these hotels are only a block or two away and feature attractions that certainly warrant a detour.

Motown display at the Hard Rock

The Hard Rock Hotel

Voted as one of the coolest places to stay in the world, the Hard Rock Hotel is a rock 'n' roll paradise. Located just east of the Las Vegas Strip on Paradise Road, the Hard Rock is also home to the celebrated music venue The Joint, which regularly features performances from rock legends such as Aerosmith and Blondie. With 670 rooms the Hard Rock may be smaller than some of its Strip competitors, but this venue wins out with style. In keeping with Hard Rock Cafés around the world, this hotel showcases a bountiful display of rock 'n' roll memorabilia from the 1950s until the present day, with artefacts from stars including Mick Jagger, Jimi Hendrix, Elvis Presley, Madonna and Britney Spears.

The Las Vegas Hilton

Also on Paradise Road, the Las Vegas Hilton was the largest hotel in the world when it opened as the International Hotel in 1969. It is famed

Masquerade Show in the Sky at the Rio

Rolling Stones memorabilia at the Hard Rock Hotel

as the Las Vegas home of Elvis Presley, where he played throughout the 1970s. As well as a mecca for Elvis fans, the Hilton is now a trekkies' paradise showcasing *Star Trek: The Experience*, a $70-million attraction that transports you to the 24th century. Some of the guest rooms have a good view of the Strip, but a northeast view over Sunrise Mountain is certainly worth requesting.

Rio

With its vibrant exterior lighting, this Brazilian-themed resort can be seen towering behind the west side of the Strip. The 2,500 guest rooms in this hotel are all suites, with floor-to-ceiling windows offering spectacular views of the Strip or the mountains. Guests can also relax in the Ipanema Beach Club, a multi-level pool complex with waterfalls and bay areas. Renegade magicians Penn and Teller have recently taken up residence at the Rio, and the resort is also famed for the *Masquerade Show in the Sky*, a free attraction that takes place in the hotel's Masquerade Village with carnival entertainers all performing on themed floats suspended on an overhead track, as stages drop down from above and come up from the floor level. For a small fee you can even join the cast. The Rio also showcases Bevertainers, singing cocktail waitresses who perform shows every ten to fifteen minutes.

Palms

On a more adult theme and almost opposite the Rio on West Flamingo Road, Palms is a popular location for bachelor and bachelorette parties. The nightlife includes the Ghost Bar, known for offering the best view of the Strip, the multi-level nightclub and concert venue Rain in the Desert and the pool party Skin. The new Playpen suites include dance floors and dance poles for the ultimate party.

Almost 90 per cent of Las Vegas visitors will gamble. They will spend around $500 each trip and take refuge for three to four hours a day in the casino. Of course, there are those who visit Las Vegas with the sole purpose of gambling, placing thousands of dollars in the casinos' hands as they win, but ultimately lose, for days on end. Then there is the professional gambler, planning to win big in poker or conquer the casinos with blackjack strategy.

Customers are rewarded in Las Vegas. Whether you are on a slot machine or in a high-stakes card game, drinks will be served for free, as long as you keep playing. You will have to tip your cocktail waitress, but the casino will treat you favourably in order to keep your business. Establishments may offer free food, show tickets or accommodation if they see you as a preferential customer. Known as 'comps', these benefits are calculated using your average bet, the time you spend gambling, and the expected house profits from your play. Big-money gamblers, or high rollers, are the most coveted by casinos, who will pick up the cost of luxury suites, limousines, fine dining and entertainment.

Before you play
Any player can benefit from comps if they sign up for free players club membership. You will be

Remember the golden rules:

- do not gamble beyond your means
- never try to win back your losses
- set a budget for gambling and stick to it.

given a card, similar in design to a credit card, which can be placed in slot or video machines as you play and also used in table games to earn points, which can be redeemed for a variety of benefits. As large corporations operate many of the Las Vegas casinos, points can be earned or redeemed throughout the group.

Most casinos will offer gaming lessons for free, particularly for complicated table games such as craps. Tuition is also offered on television channels and information on playing casino games can often be found in your hotel room or in the playing area. Before you visit Las Vegas, the easiest way to learn is on a computer game.

On the Internet, online casinos and gaming sites also offer tuition and games to download for free, but do not be coaxed into playing games using your credit card.

Opposite: Balloon advertising Paris attractions
Below: Frantic slot play in Las Vegas

Casino games

You must be over 21 years of age to gamble in Las Vegas. Visitors under this age are also prohibited from loitering in or around any area where any licensed gaming is conducted and cannot play, place bets or collect winnings.

Slot machines

Slot machines were originally used in Las Vegas to keep wives entertained while the men concentrated on the more serious table games. Now they make more money than any of the table games and, linked throughout giant networks, they offer state-wide jackpots, which rise to millions.

Las Vegas has traditional slot machines, with lines of fruit or gold bars, as well as themed machines that feature stars such as Frank Sinatra or Elvis Presley, alongside television shows, classic movies or board games such as Monopoly. Most casinos have machines with play ranging from 5¢ to $5, with the most popular being the 25¢, or quarter, slot machines. You often have to play more lines, or submit bigger stakes, to win the higher jackpots, but the returns on these machines are certainly generous enough to keep your attention.

More slot machines than you can shake a stick at!

Blackjack

This popular table game places the players against the dealer who all try to get their cards to total 21, or as close to it, without going over.

Each player is given two cards, usually face up, and then the dealer gives himself two cards with only one face up. When you total the cards in your hand, aces count as one or eleven, picture cards count as ten and all others are counted at face value.

When the dealer gives you the option of more cards you can ask to be 'hit' (receive another card) or you can 'stand', if you believe that you are as close to 21 as you can get. You can be hit as many times as you like, but if you go over 21 you 'bust' and lose your bet. After every player has finished this procedure the dealer turns his second card over and tries to reach 21. If a player is closer to 21 than the dealer, he wins an amount equal to his original bet. A player who has exactly 21, or 'blackjack', receives 3–2 odds on his bet. If both the dealer and player have 21, it's known as a 'push' and nobody wins, but if the dealer busts all players will win.

Craps

This exciting dice game involves the outcome of two dice, with players usually betting against the appearance of a seven. Most casinos offer tuition in this game, which is advisable for first-time players, as it appears very complicated when you watch it, but the basics are fairly simple when learned. Craps games are controlled by two dealers, who watch the bets and play, a stickman who collects the dice, and a boxman who oversees the play and personnel. As in any casino game, make sure that you remember to tip the dealers, or place a bet for them, as they are often your allies in successful play.

Slot machines have coloured lights on top, so you can see their denomination from a distance.

Red:	5¢ (nickels)
Yellow:	25¢ (quarters)
Gold:	50¢
Blue:	dollars

Keno

Keno could be described as a lottery game. Nevada does not have a state lottery but keno games can be played every few minutes, in casinos, restaurants and even from your hotel room. Players choose between 1 and 15 numbers from 80 numbers on the keno form, and submit the ticket. When the game is played, a winning combination can result in some very generous winnings. Like any lottery, it is very easy to participate, but the odds are rarely in your favour.

Roulette

Portrayed as one of the more glamorous casino games, players try to predict the outcome of the roulette wheel. As it spins, a ball races round in the opposite direction coming to a halt in one of 38 numbered red or black slots on the wheel. When the croupier announces that players should place their bets, chips can be placed on numbers from 1 through to 36, zero, or double zero. More favourable odds can be achieved, but for much smaller returns, by betting simply that the ball will land on red or black, or an odd or even number, or between a range of numbers indicated on the roulette table. When the croupier announces there are no more bets, players wait to see where the ball settles. After the number is announced all winning bets are paid and all other chips go to the house.

Poker

Las Vegas poker is a game of skill and certainly not for the novice. Unless you have played before and know what you are doing, it is best to leave the tables well alone. Games played in Vegas include Seven Card Stud, Texas Hold 'Em, Omaha, Omaha Hi Low, Five Card Draw and Low Ball, while house rules vary in different casinos. For beginners, the easiest way to play poker is on a video machine or the card game Pai Gow. However, poker is rapidly becoming very popular away from the casino and many new satellite television channels offer tips and tuition to master the game.

Video Poker

With many variations such as Jacks or Better, Deuces Wild and Bonus Poker, video poker can certainly be one of the most enjoyable, but addictive, machine games in Las Vegas. If you know the basic principles of poker then it's very easy to play. You are dealt five cards on the screen and then have the choice of

which cards to keep and which to change. To keep cards, you can press the hold buttons below the screen, or touch the display to hold them, then the remaining cards are dealt again and winning cards are rewarded. The machines usually display the payout for each type of hand, which beginners can also use as a reference to learn the game. Expert players can play multiple hands at once.

Pai Gow Poker

Not to be confused with Pai Gow, which is played with coloured tiles, Pai Gow poker is a card game where up to six players can play against the dealer. Like video poker, if you know the ranking of poker hands, Pai Gow can be a very enjoyable and relatively easy game to learn. Players are dealt seven cards, which they split into two hands, one with five cards and one with two. To win, both your hands should beat the dealer's, and if you win one each, it is regarded as 'push' or a draw. Overall, Pai Gow is a friendly game. The dealer can help you arrange your cards and the other players are not competing against you.

Baccarat

This game is often associated with high rollers, who have been known to bet hundreds of thousands on a single hand. However, if you find the table limit within your price range this game is very easy to play. To win, the value of your cards must reach eight or nine. You can bet on the player or banker to win, or bet on a draw. The banker is the person that holds the shoe, which contains the playing cards and remains in their possession while the banker's hand is winning. Picture cards and tens are counted as zero, ace counts as one and other cards are taken at face value. If the total of your cards reaches two

digits the first number is ignored. For example, if you had a five and an eight, your total would be three (thirteen, without the first digit). More cards can be drawn according to baccarat rules, and there is a small commission payable on banker bets.

Below: A slot machine plays tribute to Ol' Blue Eyes

Downtown

The city of Las Vegas is barely 100 years old. While the Strip populates the south end of Las Vegas Boulevard, if you follow the road just a couple of miles north – past the Stratosphere and a profusion of wedding chapels – a collection of vintage neon signs will welcome you Downtown: to Fremont Street, Main Street and Glitter Gulch. This is where it all started.

It was here in 1905 that the city, fortified by the railroad from Los Angeles to Salt Lake City, was founded. It was later boosted by the construction of the Hoover Dam, the end of prohibition, and legalised gambling. After Downtown started to develop, the first hotels appeared on the Strip, shifting the focus of tourism to the south of the city.

From the northern end of the Strip, how many visitors have looked out from their hotel rooms at that twinkling spot in the distance, and wondered what is out there? The answer is simple – Downtown Las Vegas.

The original Downtown area was once the bustling centre of the city and has now been redeveloped as a celebrated new tourist attraction, with street entertainers, antique neon signs and a unique light show known as the *Fremont Street Experience*.

This area is also home to many famous Las Vegas establishments, such as the Golden Gate Hotel, which opened as the Hotel Nevada in 1906. At the time, rooms in this frontier-style hotel cost $1 and 24 years before gambling was legalised there was not even a casino on the premises. The Golden Gate is also famed for its shrimp cocktails, an appetiser it claims to have introduced to Las Vegas in the 1950s.

Next door on Fremont Street stands the glittering Golden Nugget, with its

The Plaza Hotel at the tip of Fremont Street

plush white and gold interior. On secure display in the lobby is the *Hand of Faith*, the world's largest gold nugget. Worth a cool million, this rock was discovered in Australia in 1980. The hotel is also famed for its buffet and is a popular gambling spot for visitors and locals. Just outside its doors, you have the optimum viewing point for the *Fremont Street Experience*.

The Fremont Hotel and the Four Queens

Across the street is Binion's Gambling Hall and Hotel, known as the legendary Horseshoe. In 1946 the enterprising Benny Binion moved to Las Vegas from Texas then opened this establishment four years later. The casino is famed for its no-limit gambling, which Binion pioneered in the city along with the 'comps' system as he worked hard to reward and encourage gamblers, regardless of their budget. The casino is also famed for presenting the World Series of Poker, where for an ante of $10,000 players can compete for the ultimate poker accolade and one million dollars in cash. Dark and smoky, Binion's does have the ambience of a serious gambling den.

From the Strip, the Deuce bus route will take you Downtown.

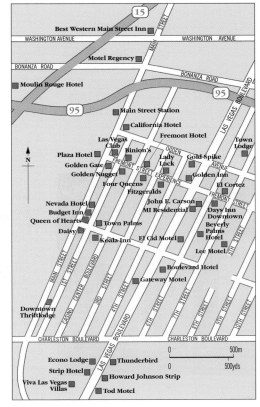

The Fremont Street Experience

One of the must-see sights of your visit, the *Fremont Street Experience* started as a $70-million collaboration between the city of Las Vegas and Downtown casinos, and has already evolved considerably.

Glitter Gulch

Before the attraction opened, tourists were always lured to the Strip area and Downtown Las Vegas was almost forgotten. Now the area has been completely rejuvenated to become an award-winning tourist attraction.

Located between Las Vegas Boulevard and Main Street, this four-block section includes Las Vegas originals such as Binion's Gambling Hall and Hotel, the California Hotel, Fitzgerald's, the Four Queens, Fremont Hotel, Lady Luck Casino, the Las Vegas Club, Main Street Station Casino, the Golden Gate and Golden Nugget. This street is much

Dazzling Fremont Street

smaller than the Strip with its six lanes of busy traffic. The area has been completely pedestrianised, and it's easy to visit all Fremont Street establishments.

Running four blocks over Fremont Street is the 27m (90ft) high canopy *Viva Vision: The Biggest Big Screen on the Planet*. Previous visitors to Downtown Las Vegas will remember the $70-million *Fremont Street Experience* light show, which was presented on this canopy, until a $17-million expansion in 2004 created the world's largest graphic display system, longer than five football fields.

Set to music, animated displays offer shows that include a girls' night out in *Downtown Days*, cars tearing along the length of the canopy in *Speed, Smoke and Spinning Wheels*, an Alien Encounter in *Area 51*, and *Lucky Vegas*, created to celebrate the city's 100th birthday.

The state-of-the-art LED canopy technology incorporates 12.5 million bulbs, 220 amplifiers capable of producing 550,000 watts of concert-quality sound, 180 high-intensity strobe lights, 64 variable lighting fixtures that can produce more than 300 different colours, 7,000-watt skytrackers and robotic mirrors that pan and tilt to reflect light.

As each show starts, the businesses on Fremont Street dim their lights and everyone stops still, transfixed by the show above them. Between performances, the area bustles with street entertainers and live music, while you can browse the retail kiosks on the street.

In its formative years Downtown Las Vegas was nicknamed Glitter Gulch, and you will certainly understand this title when you visit. Unlike the computerised façades on the Strip, Fremont Street radiates with neon, and you can feel the warmth of its glow. The area is also home to the Neon Sign Museum. Many well-known Vegas signs are displayed in this area, including the cowgirl Vegas Vicki and her Marlboro-like suitor Vegas Vic (*see pp90–91 & 92–3*).

The Fremont Street Experience, 425 Fremont Street. Tel: (702) 678 5777. Viva Vision shows are performed on the hour from 6pm until midnight (although this may vary depending on the time of year). There is no admission charge for this attraction and most people stand in the street to watch the show. Restaurant and food prices are very competitive on Fremont Street compared to the Strip.

The Fremont Street area is safe for tourists, but be watchful of your belongings when you are distracted by the show. It is advisable not to walk Downtown away from the main streets surrounding the attraction area. If you are driving, valet parking at the Golden Nugget is recommended.

Vegas Vicki

Neonopolis

For its wealth of luminous signs, the ever-expanding metropolitan area of Las Vegas has often been nicknamed Neonopolis. Along the Strip, computerised billboards compete for your attention, while brilliant high-tech advertisements tower above you, although Downtown Las Vegas seems to have a brighter, warmer glow. It's in this area, on Fremont Street between Main and Las Vegas Boulevard, that you can view the original Las Vegas greetings and the most recognisable symbol for the desert city: Vegas Vic.

Vegas Vic

Vegas Vic was created by the Young Electric Sign Company and erected on top of the Pioneer Club in 1951. This mechanical cowboy was a trusted promotional tool for Las Vegas as his 'Howdy Pardner' greeting had been used across matchbooks, postcards and advertisements since the Second World War. In its time, Vegas Vic was the largest mechanical sign in the world, as its arm waved a welcome to visiting tourists. If you tried to get a good night's sleep in the area, it was likely to be disturbed by Vic's oft-repeated catchphrase.

Thomas Young Senior created YESCO in 1920, then in 1931 when gambling was legalised he travelled through the Las Vegas area and saw an open marketplace, which his company would later dominate. Designing most of the famed signs in the city, Thomas Young worked from his own sketches and many of his creations still line the streets Downtown, where they are featured in a 4.8-km (3-mile) Neon Museum that showcases vintage signs from the heyday of Las Vegas. The Hacienda horse and rider, which once glistened upon the site where Mandalay Bay now stands, has been restored Downtown along with the sparkling magic lamp from the original

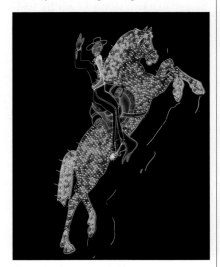

The Hacienda Horse and Rider

Aladdin Hotel, in a radiant presentation of vintage neon signs with many more classics still in the restoration process.

Today, Las Vegas is dominated by computerised signs, with Fremont Street's Viva Vision towering over Vegas Vic and Thomas Young's other original creations.

The name Neonopolis has now been adopted by a 18,580sq m (200,000sq ft) entertainment complex, modelled after San Diego's Horton Plaza. Three storeys high and emblazoned with neon, the building is home to Crown 14, a multi-plex cinema with some of the largest screens in the area at very competitive prices. There are video games and bowling, shopping areas and the Courtyard Tower, with more displays of antique neon signs. Every taste is catered for with restaurants such as

Jillian's, La Salsa and The Saloon along with a food court featuring a wide selection of fast-food outlets.

The Neon Museum is located on Fremont Street between Main Street and Las Vegas Boulevard. The displays can be viewed for free, but will be far more impressive by night. There are also plaques that explain the history of each sign.

Neonopolis is located at the east end of the *Fremont Street Experience* where Fremont Street meets Las Vegas Boulevard. *450 Fremont Street. Tel: (702) 477 0470. Open: Sun–Thur 11am–9.30pm (food court closes 7pm), Fri–Sat 11am–10pm (food court closes 9pm).*

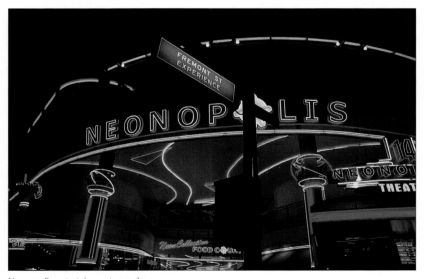

Neonopolis entertainment complex

Tour: Glitter Gulch

The best time to see Downtown Las Vegas in all its glory is by night. Known as Glitter Gulch, the best and most sparkling attractions are all free and all contained within an area that can easily be walked in a short space of time. *Allow one evening. You can reach Downtown from the Strip using the Deuce bus service.*

1 The Neon Museum

Carefully restored, the Neon Museum starts at the end of the *Fremont Street Experience* canopy where the road meets Las Vegas Boulevard. From here, take a walking tour of the signs along the length of Fremont Street. The **Hacienda Horse and Rider**, the first display on this intersection, once stood outside the Hacienda on the Strip, where it was

installed in 1967. **Aladdin's Lamp** first appeared on the original Aladdin Hotel when it opened in 1966. The **Flame Restaurant** sign was installed on the Desert Inn Road in 1961. The **Chief Hotel Court** sign on the northwest corner of 4th Street was originally installed on East Fremont Street in 1940. Opposite, **Andy Anderson**, the playful mascot for the Anderson Dairy, was installed in 1956 on their premises on Las Vegas Boulevard. Dating from the 1940s, the original location for the **Wedding Information** sign is unknown. **Red Barn** dates around 1960, but although the sign was saved the Red Barn bar on Tropicana Avenue burnt down. Dating around 1950, the **Nevada Motel** sign features the first appearance of Vegas Vic. **Dot's Flowers** was originally located on Las Vegas Boulevard in the 1940s, while

---

Map labels:

WASHINGTON AVENUE — WASHINGTON AVENUE
Motel Regency
BONANZA ROAD
BONANZA ROAD
15
95
Main Street Station
3
California Hotel
Las Vegas Club
Fremont Hotel
Binion's
Town Lodge
Plaza Hotel
4
Golden Gate
4
FREMONT STREET
OGDEN
Lady Luck
Gold Spike
AVENUE
Golden Nugget
EXPERIENCE STREET
Golden Inn
Four Queens
Fitzgeralds
The Neon Museum
1
El Cortez
FREMONT STREET
Nevada Hotel
John E. Carson
Budget Inn
MJ Residential
Days Inn Downtown
Queen of Hearts
Town Palms
Beverly Palms Hotel
Daisy
El Cid Motel
Koala Inn
Lee Motel
LAS VEGAS BOULEVARD
7TH STREET
9TH STREET
N
0   500m
0   500yds

Binion's Gambling Hall and Hotel

5th Street Liquor was a Downtown establishment on Las Vegas Boulevard, where this sign dates from 1946.

Open: 24 hours. New additions are always made to this museum, which offers more exhibits in Neonopolis. Continue west along Fremont Street.

2 Viva Vision

Browse Fremont Street establishments such as the Four Queens, Fitzgerald's or the Golden Nugget until the light show starts at the top of every hour. There are also traders and entertainers in the street, and you can enjoy live music (local magazines will list the current entertainment schedule). Most people stand to watch the show, but for a more comfortable view, grab a coffee and sit outside Starbucks at the Golden Nugget.

Go to the end of Fremont Street and turn right onto Main Street.

3 Main Street Station

Make sure you find the time to see the unusual antiques and memorabilia in this casino, which include curiosities such as Theodore Roosevelt's railroad car and a section of the Berlin Wall. Stop in at the Triple 7 Brew Pub and sample their speciality beers, oysters or garlic-and-herb French fries.

Main Street Station, 200 North Main Street. Retrace your steps back along Main Street, and turn left onto Fremont Street.

4 Binion's Coffee Shop

For a late stop and some of the best steaks in town call in at *Binion's Coffee Shop*. Otherwise, for an unrivalled view of Fremont Street, visit the *Upper Deck Restaurant* at the Plaza at the tip of Fremont Street, where it meets Main Street. Home to the world-famous 9lb *Big Daddy Barrick Burger*, which the Plaza challenges any individual to eat within 24 hours to earn a place in their Hall of Fame.

Binion's Coffee Shop is open 24 hours in Binion's Gambling Hall and Hotel, 128 Fremont St.

The Upper Deck restaurant is open 24 hours at the Plaza Hotel and Casino, 1 Main St.

… and directly opposite, the Golden Nugget

Las Vegas origins

North of Fremont Street, just a few blocks from Vegas Vic, the Golden Nugget and a multi-million-dollar light show, stands an old Mormon fort. It is protected within a State Historic Park, quite tiny in comparison to other national treasures, but represents the place where Las Vegas began.

Where it all started

For thousands of years, a small oasis in the middle of the desert supplied water for travellers, and was a meeting point for the native Paiute. The underground source was 6km (4 miles) away, but the water bubbled to the surface and formed a small creek and river that disappeared into the desert. The area was named *Las Vegas*, or 'the meadows', and in 1855 a team of Mormon missionaries built the first permanent structure on the desert landscape. A fort was built from sun-dried bricks under the leadership of William Bringhurst, and it served as a post office and resting point for travellers, heavily guarded with 45-m (150-ft) walls and two lookout towers. With the creek's resources they grew crops and tended an orchard, but abandoned the fort due to harsh desert temperatures and discord within the group.

In 1865 Octavius D Gass occupied the land. Using materials from the abandoned fort he built a ranch house, and ran a blacksmith's forge and a store that sold beef, vegetables and fruit. He financed his land purchases with a loan from Archibald Stewart at an extortionate 30 per cent interest rate, which Gass was unable to meet – so in 1881 the ranch became the possession of his creditor. Three years later, Archibald's wife Helen Stewart inherited the 720 hectares (1,800 acres) after her lover murdered her husband during a so-called act of self-defence.

As a main rail line was planned for the state, Helen Stewart predicted a

The original downtown hotel

boom in the desert area. She hired civil engineer James McWilliams, who made large land purchases and sold lots to the west of the proposed rail line, creating the original Las Vegas town site in 1904. Reaching Las Vegas in 1905, the rail line was owned by Senator William Clark, who created a new town plan on the east side of the line instead. Over 3,000 prospective buyers attended Clark's public auction, while many of the original residents simply picked up their wooden properties and dragged them across the rail tracks to the new Las Vegas on the east. With credit to Clark, the thriving new city of Las Vegas was officially founded in 1905.

Today, the Old Las Vegas Mormon Fort is open to the public. The ranch house no longer exists, but part of the fort still remains and there are replicas of pioneer gardens, a corral and a museum detailing the history of the site. In 1929 part of the fort was used as a concrete testing lab for the construction of the Hoover Dam.

Old Las Vegas Mormon Fort, 500 East Washington Ave. Tel: (702) 486 3511. The park is open daily 8.30am–4.30pm. Admission is inexpensive and there are guided tours at 11am and 1pm. There is no charge for children under six.

The corral at the Old Las Vegas Fort

Tour: Historic Las Vegas

Although the city is still rapidly developing, there are many historic sites left in Las Vegas, some of which are listed on the National Register of Historic Places.

Allow one day.

Many of these sights are located around the Downtown area of Las Vegas. Sights 2–6 can be reached on foot from Fremont Street, but to reach the rest of the sights you will need your own car or other transport. You can reach Downtown from the Strip using the Deuce bus service.

1 The Old Las Vegas Mormon Fort

Start your tour in the area of the Las Vegas Creek where the Mormon missionaries built their adobe fort in 1855. Parts of the original fort still remain and there is a museum with information on the succeeding occupants and the founding of Las Vegas.
500 East Washington Ave.
CAT bus route 113 runs up Las Vegas Boulevard to Washington Ave from the Downtown Transportation Center on Stewart Ave.

2 Victory Hotel

This is the oldest remaining Downtown hotel. It was built in 1910 and was a stop for railroad employees and passengers.
307 South Main Street.
Head north on Main Street and turn right onto Fremont Street.

3 Golden Gate Hotel and Casino

First opened in 1906 as Hotel Nevada, later to be renamed Sal Sagev. If you are puzzled by this name, read it backwards.
1 Fremont Street.
Continue along Fremont Street.

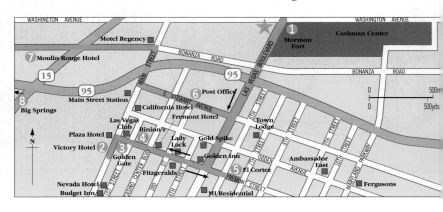

4 Apache Hotel and Binion's Gambling Hall and Hotel

Opened in 1931, the Apache Hotel was described as the plushest hotel in the city. It's still tucked behind Binion's, which has been on Fremont Street since 1951.

128 Fremont Street.
Continue in the same direction along Fremont Street until just past the junction with 6th Street.

5 El Cortez Hotel & Casino

Built in 1941 for $245,000, this was the first major resort in Las Vegas and today its exterior remains unaltered.

600 Fremont Street.
Head back west along Fremont Street and turn right on Las Vegas Blvd. Continue along until you reach East Stewart Ave, then turn left.

El Cortez was the first Las Vegas resort

6 Post Office/Federal Building

This impressive building just behind Fremont Street was built in 1933. It is now home to a new cultural centre including a mob exhibit championed by Mayor Oscar Goodman.

301 East Stewart Ave.

7 The Moulin Rouge Hotel & Casino

Listed on the National Register of Historic Places, the Moulin Rouge opened in 1955 and was the first desegregated casino in Las Vegas. It is not open to the public, but is a great example of the resort architecture appearing in Las Vegas in the '50s.

900 West Bonanza Road.
CAT bus route 214/215 runs past the Moulin Rouge from the Downtown Transportation Center on Stewart Ave. Note: you cannot enter the property and it is not advisable to stop in this area.

8 Big Springs

Where John Fremont recorded the discovery of Las Vegas. These springs provided all the water for Las Vegas until Lake Mead was used as a resource.

Valley View Blvd, between Alta Drive and US 95.

Outside Las Vegas in Henderson, the Clark County Heritage Museum details the area's history including Boulder City, Las Vegas and the formation of Henderson as a location for bomb production in the Second World War. The museum includes restored buildings among its fascinating artefacts.
Clark County Heritage Museum,
1820 South Boulder Highway, Henderson.
Tel: (702) 455 7955.

Las Vegas is famed as a popular honeymoon destination where 125,000 couples get married every year. You can choose from 24-hour drive-through services, golf-club retreats, luxurious resort packages or even weddings by helicopter. Prospective partners simply purchase a licence from the Clark County Courthouse in Las Vegas. You need to produce proof of age and ID, proof of divorce if necessary, and under-16s need written parental consent. The courthouse is open until midnight on weekdays and 24 hours at the weekend – it is almost too easy.

With your licence in hand, almost every hotel in Las Vegas can offer you a wedding package. You can choose a French Victorian wedding service at the Monte Carlo, a medieval service at the Canterbury Wedding Chapels at the Excalibur, or you can take a vow to live long and prosper on board the USS *Enterprise* at the Hilton. You can marry by the beach at Mandalay Bay, head for the heights for a wedding in the sky at the Stratosphere tower, or take advantage of one of the independent wedding chapels in the city.

There are countless wedding chapels in Las Vegas. Many of these are located towards the North of the Strip near the Stratosphere, which is where you can find the Little Church Of Las Vegas. Despite its name, this is actually the largest wedding chapel in Las Vegas and packages include their *Fairy Tale Wedding*, which features the bride's grand entrance in a fairy-tale coach pulled by footmen.

If you want to wed away from the Strip, the Little Church of the West is located at the southern tip of Las Vegas Boulevard. Based on an old mining-town church,

the chapel is the oldest structure left on the Las Vegas Strip and was the first wedding chapel in the area when it was originally located on the grounds of the Last Frontier in 1942. Its first of many celebrity weddings was the marriage of Zsa Zsa Gabor to George Saunders in 1943, and since then Las Vegas has become known as a wedding destination for the stars, with marriages that have included Frank Sinatra and Mia Farrow, Elvis Presley and Priscilla Beaulieu, Jane Fonda and Roger Vadim, Bruce Willis and Demi Moore, Cindy Crawford and Richard Gere, and Billy Bob Thornton and Angelina Jolie.

Another Las Vegas tradition is to have Elvis at your wedding, a service offered by many wedding chapels such as the Graceland Chapel or Viva Las Vegas Wedding Chapel, as well as many resort chapels in the city.

Weddings can range in price from a few hundred dollars to several thousands in Las Vegas, and you can preview many Las Vegas chapels on the internet where you can also view live weddings. Most hotels will offer wedding packages to include your honeymoon. In general, independent wedding chapels are cheaper than hotels, but allow for extra costs, which may include:
- DVD or cassette recording of your ceremony
- use of the chapel or the services of the minister
- live or recorded music
- fresh or artificial flowers
- transport

There is also a charge for the marriage licence.

Opposite: A drive-through wedding chapel
Above: The Little Church of the West is the oldest structure on the Strip

Time to relax

With nearly four miles of casinos and 24-hour entertainment on the Strip, the blaze of neon in Fremont Street and the endless soundtrack of tinkling fruit machines, after visiting Las Vegas you may need another holiday to recover. However, this is a city that has thought of everything and there are many more ways to relax than just soaking up the sun, or simply sipping cocktails.

Stairway to Bellagio Spa

Spas and health clubs

Americans make over 150 million visits to a spa each year and there are over 30 of these retreats in Las Vegas. At the Hard Rock Hotel you can enjoy facials, aromatherapy and a body massage at the Rock Spa, or indulge in water therapy and massage at the three-storey spa at the Palms, while the Canyon Ranch Spa Club at the Venetian was recently voted one of the top ten spas in America by *Condé Nast Traveler* magazine.

Most major hotels have spa facilities, which can include massage, wraps, herbal baths and body treatments such as shiatsu or reflexology. They usually include swimming pools, fitness rooms, steam rooms, saunas and whirlpools, while offering several hair and beauty treatments, manicures and pedicures or classes such as pilates and yoga. You may be offered discount rates at your hotel spa if you are a guest, but many spa facilities are open to the public as well as to hotel residents.

Outside Las Vegas, there are award-winning spas at Lake Las Vegas, Laughlin and Mesquite, where you can try several New-Age therapies such as

reiki life energy alignment and cranio-sacral therapy.

Golf

Take a day out from the tables at one of the area's award-winning golf courses. There are over 60 courses around Las Vegas and many of these are championship courses with breathtaking views and landscaping. It's hard to believe you are just a few short miles from the city, or maybe even secluded within it, as is the case at Bali Hai – where, with swaying palm trees over white crushed granite, you feel as if you are in the South Pacific rather than at the south end of the Strip. On West Flamingo Avenue, Bear's Best golf course was designed by legendary golfer Jack Nicklaus, and the views take in the dramatic Red Rock Mountains as well as a paramount view of the Las Vegas skyline. *See pp156–7.*

Take a side trip

There are many attractions and state parks just a short distance away from Las Vegas. Take time out to visit Laughlin, Mesquite, Henderson, Primm or Jean. If you want to escape the casinos completely, try Boulder City, originally founded to house workers for the Hoover Dam, where gambling is still prohibited. Relax at Lake Mead or take a tour of the dam (*see pp112–13*), or see nature at her most inspiring with a visit to the Grand Canyon (*see pp104–9*).

As hotel prices and occupancy tend to rise in Las Vegas over the weekend, you should plan your trip to visit other areas in Nevada, or head in the opposite direction to the traffic and drive out to California, where you could be in Disneyland or Hollywood in five to six hours.

The spa at the Mirage

getting away

The surrounding area

Las Vegas is nestled in the southern tip of Nevada, close to the California, Utah and Arizona borders and the expansive Nellis Air Force Range to the north. This area is home to many state parks and attractions and close to the Grand Canyon National Park, while there are several other satellite cities all within a short drive of Las Vegas.

Laughlin

Laughlin

Situated on the banks of the Colorado, this new city was founded by Don Laughlin in 1966, when he purchased a run-down motel and transformed it into the Riverside Resort Hotel and Casino. Located on the Nevada–Arizona border 144km (90 miles) southeast of Las Vegas, Laughlin quickly flourished into a popular tourist destination that now attracts over five million visitors a year. There are ten hotel casinos in Laughlin, seven golf courses in the area, and you can take to the Colorado in speedboats, on water skis, kayaks, canoes or the River Express, a river taxi that serves the waterfront casinos. Like its older cousin Las Vegas, Laughlin boasts an enviable

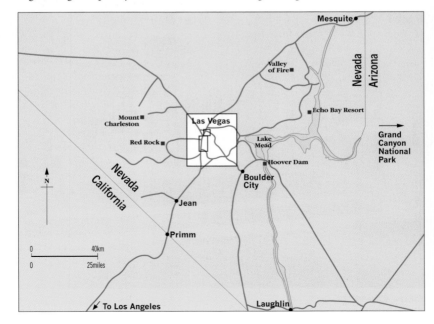

selection of restaurants, entertainment and shopping with the Art-Deco Horizon Outlet Center. On the other side of the Colorado lies the mining town of Oatman, still considered as the Wild West.

Mesquite

Another border town, Mesquite is located on Interstate 15, 128km (80 miles) to the north of Las Vegas on the Arizona border. The city was named after the mesquite tree, considered to be lucky by Native Americans, and was founded back in 1894, but only opened its first hotel casino in the 1980s. With four resorts, championship golf courses and award-winning spas, Mesquite is a wonderful retreat and the gateway to national parks in southern Utah, with the Zion National Park only two hours away.

Primm

If you drive into Las Vegas from Los Angeles on Interstate 15, Primm offers your very first glimpse of Nevada. Located on the Californian state line

56km (35 miles) from Las Vegas, after a long desert drive, its twinkling lights tempt you with your first opportunity to gamble. There are three hotel casinos in Primm: Whisky Pete's, Primm Valley Resort and Buffalo Bill's, which is also home to the theme park that boasts the *Desperado* rollercoaster. Other attractions include cars that once belonged to characters such as Bonnie and Clyde, Dutch Schultz and Al Capone, designer shopping in the Fashion Outlet of Las Vegas, and two golf courses designed by Tom Fazio.

Jean

A little further towards Las Vegas, also on Interstate 15, is Jean, which features two themed hotels, the Gold Strike and Nevada Landing. Jean is also home to the Las Vegas Convention and Visitors Authority.

Boulder City

Built to house the 5,000 workers on the Boulder Dam Project, Boulder City is the only city in Nevada where gambling is illegal. Approximately 50km (30 miles) outside Las Vegas, Boulder City overlooks Lake Mead and offers several recreational activities, scenic parks and a museum that details the human story behind the construction of the dam, which is only 11km (7 miles) away.

Boulder City's historic district

The Grand Canyon

This awe-inspiring sight lies in the Colorado Plateau within northwest Arizona. Formed over millions of years, the Grand Canyon is a huge natural chasm 445km (277 miles) long and 1.6km (1 mile) deep. Carved by the great Colorado River, the canyon offers one of the most spectacular examples of erosion anywhere in the world. Each layer of rock provides a record of the earth's geological history and it is speculated that the rocks at the bottom of the canyon may be two billion years old.

View from the North Rim

TOURS

There are many theories to explain the existence of the Canyon. The area was once a vast mountainous region – the top has been flattened by the forces of nature, but the 1.7-billion-year-old bases of the mountains still exist. Limestone layers such as Redwall Limestone (330 million years old) and Muav Limestone (530 million years old) provide evidence that the area was once underwater, while layers like the Hermit Shale (280 million years old) contain fossils of land-based plants. Changes in the earth's orbit over millions of years caused climatic changes, making the water retreat and advance to create the distinctive coloured layers visible in the Canyon. Other geological factors such as continental drift and the subsequent volcanic and seismic activity also played a huge role in the Canyon's formation and created the younger rock formations found in the Bryce and Zion Canyons. Then 60–70 million years ago the Rocky Mountains were formed, and the Colorado River began its flow. When the Colorado Plateau began to lift upwards, the river changed course and started to carve out the Grand Canyon, exposing the geological history of the area.

Several tour operators offer trips to the Grand Canyon. Most popular are the flight tours from Las Vegas, lasting from a few hours to the whole day. You can fly down early in the morning, see the sunrise and stop for brunch on the edge of the canyon then return before midday, or spend a whole day in the park, visit Indian reservations and see the sun set.

The two main visitor areas are the North and South Rims of the Canyon, offering breathtaking vistas of raised plateaus

Gran

• Tuweep

Hualapai Indian
Reservation

and steep-walled canyons, stunning views that will far outrival any other natural formation of this kind. By car, the South Rim (where the visitor centre is located) is approximately 432km (270 miles) from Las Vegas, while the North Rim is 416km (260 miles). Across the canyon the two rims are only 16km (10 miles) away from each other, but by road they are separated by 344km (215 miles).

For hikers, the canyon provides over 640km (400 miles) of trails and there are many camping and lodge facilities available. Make sure that you make your reservations early, particularly on the South Rim where activities and lodgings can be booked well in advance. Both of these rims are at a very high altitude so all activity will be strenuous, even walking.

South of the Colorado lies the Havasupai Indian Reservation, which can only by reached by horseback or a 13-km (8-mile) hike, while the Hualapai Indian Reservation is further west.

WILDLIFE

The Grand Canyon supports many rare plant and animal species, some of which are unique to the area. Its ecosystem creates an environment as diverse as the area stretching between Canada and Mexico, as the canyon provides five out of seven life zones identified in the United States: the Lower Sonoran, Upper Sonoran, Transition, Canadian and Hudsonian.

The Grand Canyon is home to over 1,500 plant species along with 355 birds, 89 mammals, 47 reptiles, 9 amphibians and 17 species of fish. Highlights include the endangered humpbacked chub, found only in the Colorado River system and the largest land bird in America, the

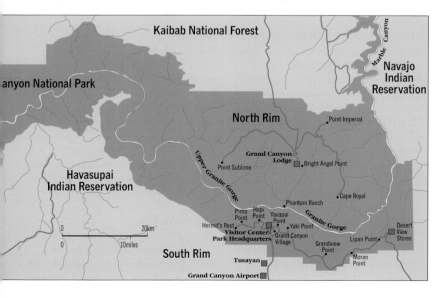

The North Rim of the Grand Canyon

California condor, a member of the vulture family. Other birds and mammals include owls, hummingbirds, woodpeckers, bats, squirrels, bighorn sheep, mountain lions, wild burros, porcupines and skunks.

It is illegal to feed or approach wild animals, especially deer and squirrels, as this threatens their environment and they may become addicted to human food. Avoid all wild animals: deer can kick and squirrels often bite eager tourists. The park imposes fines of up to $5,000 for anyone caught feeding or disturbing the animals, and if you see anyone breaking these rules, advise them to stop, or notify the park authorities.

CLIMATE
The South Rim
In the summer, temperatures are generally 10°–26°C (50°–80°F), while in the winter ice may affect the roads or trails and there will be some closures due to snow. Temperatures at these times can range from −1° to −18°C (30° to 0°F). During the spring and autumn the weather can be very changeable, so check weather forecasts when you plan your visit.

The North Rim
At a slightly higher elevation than the South Rim, temperatures here are a little cooler. Highway 67, leading to the North Rim, is closed during the winter.

Snow can also appear at any time of year on this rim. Both rims are prone to afternoon rain.

Inside the Canyon

In the summer, the inner canyon can be extremely hot and, as you descend, the temperature rises. It can reach over 49°C (120°F) by the river.

THE SOUTH RIM

With an elevation of 2,100m (7,000ft) above sea level, the South Rim of the canyon is 432km (270 miles) from Las Vegas by car. The Grand Canyon National Park attracts over five million visitors every year so prepare for this popular lookout point to be very busy in the summer months. Quieter times to visit would be from November until February but winter weather may affect your visit.

Point Imperial, view of Mount Hayden

SAFETY

When visiting the Grand Canyon, follow safety guidelines issued by the park authorities.

- Stay on the trails and avoid the edges. Only take vehicles and bicycles on maintained roads for private vehicles.
- Avoid visiting during thunderstorms.
- Wear sunscreen and protective clothing and ensure you have plenty of water.
- Be aware that the altitude will be physically demanding.

Over 250 hikers have to be rescued every year, usually due to exhaustion or dehydration. Hikers should rest, stay in the shade, drink plenty of water and wear protective clothing. Do not attempt to reach the river and return in one day.

The Canyon View Information Plaza, which is also the park headquarters, offers a bookstore, visitor centre and toilet facilities, by Yavapai Point. There are several points to view the canyon and look down towards the Colorado to the east and west of the rim, such as Hermits Rest, 13km (8 miles) to the west of the centre, which takes in Hopi and Pima Point. Known as Hermits Road, this route is usually closed to private vehicles, but a shuttle bus can take you to some of the overlooks and the route can also be walked. Some sections are paved, but run close to the rim and can be narrow in places. You are not allowed to cycle this route.

To the east of the visitor centre is Desert View Drive, which you can access by car. It follows the canyon rim for 42km (26 miles) past overlooks such as

Yaki Point, Grandview Point, Moran Point and Lipan Point just before it reaches Desert View, which has camping and food services.

The Grand Canyon Village offers food, camping and lodging facilities and the area is also served by the Grand Canyon Airport in Tusayan, which offers more facilities, and shuttles to the rim.

THE NORTH RIM
Located 416km (260 miles) from Las Vegas, the North Rim is only open from mid-May until mid-October. There is a shuttle service from the South Rim, but this journey is over 344km (215 miles). Driving in on Highway 67, the entrance to the Rim and the Grand Canyon Lodge is close to Bright Angel Point where you can look over Angel Canyon and catch a glimpse of the South Rim. The North Rim is 2,400m (8,000ft) above sea level, so the altitude can be very demanding. You tend to look over and across the canyon rather than into it, and along with the Grand Canyon Lodge area, the main lookouts include Point Imperial, where at 2,683m (8,803ft) you can see the canyon evolve from the narrow Marble Canyon to the expanse of the Grand Canyon. Beyond this, Cape Royal is a popular place to watch the sunrise and sunset and see the Colorado arch gracefully into the canyon, while Point Sublime offers a fantastic view, although you will need a 4×4 vehicle to reach it.

HOW TO GET THERE
The South Rim
By car, drive southeast on US 93 past the Hoover Dam to SR 40 east to Williams,

The mighty Colorado River

then take the 64 and 180 north to the Grand Canyon Village.

The North Rim
Drive east on Interstate 15 to SR 9 (North of St George, Utah), continue to go east, then take SR 89 south on Mount Carmel junction leading to the North Rim.

Tours
You can reach the Grand Canyon in one hour by plane or helicopter, and there are countless tours available from Las Vegas, including:
American Adventure Tours, with a huge selection of tours including the North and South Rim and Colorado Raft Tours. *Tel: (702) 876 4600.*
Maverick Helicopter Tours, with private landing areas in the Canyon. *6075 Las Vegas Blvd S. Tel: (888) 261 4414.*
www.maverickhelicopter.com;
www.americanadventuretours.com

BACKCOUNTRY AND THE COLORADO

Hiking down to the river can be described as either exhilarating or a difficult ordeal. Heading downwards in a desert environment, hikers face steep descents and rising temperatures. Then on their return they have strenuous climbs. The Grand Canyon covers over 0.5 million hectares (1.2 million acres) and includes 640km (400 miles) of hiking trails. It is not safe to try and hike to the bottom of the canyon and return in one day, so you will have to obtain a permit to stay overnight in the area. Permits need to be applied for at least four to five months in advance and spaces are limited. The park authorities want the minimum of human impact in the area and there are strict guidelines to follow.

The only place you can cross the Colorado River is at Phantom Ranch, below both the North and South Rims of the Grand Canyon. To reach the Colorado by car, you will need to drive to Lees Ferry near Marble Canyon. Activities on the Colorado include sightseeing tours and private river trips, ranging from one day on the water to a trip lasting several days. White-water rafting trips are also available.

TUWEEP

With a drop of 900m (3,000ft) into the canyon, Tuweep is located on the north side of the Colorado and with its lava flows and cinder columns it offers evidence of the volcanic activity that once took place in the area. There is camping available but the road to Tuweep is unpaved.

Helicopter tours are a popular way to visit the Grand Canyon

The Hoover Dam is one of America's seven Modern Civil Engineering wonders. Just 48km (30 miles) outside Las Vegas, the dam meets the domestic water needs of over 18 million people in Nevada, Arizona and California and also generates low-cost hydroelectric power for the same three states.

The dam is fuelled by the great Colorado River, which runs a 2,240-km (1,400-mile) course from the Colorado Rocky Mountains to the Gulf of California. During the 1800s and early 1900s the river often flooded to destroy millions of dollars' worth of crops, so a determined effort had to be made to control its flow and harness the resource it could provide.

In 1922 the Colorado River Compact divided the river among the seven states it ran through, paving the way for a series of storage dams. Six years later President Calvin Coolidge signed the Boulder Dam Project Act, and then construction began in 1931. After a previous site was found to be unsuitable, engineers settled on Black Canyon and the dam began to take shape.

A record 2.37 million cu m (3.25 million cubic yards) of concrete was poured over a four-year period, completing the dam well within budget and two years ahead of schedule. It was the most ambitious engineering project since the construction of the Panama Canal and provided work for an influx of new residents who signed up for the project as the country recovered from the Great Depression. As gambling was legalised in Nevada, the city of Las Vegas boomed with the dam's construction, although the project management soon put

THE UNITED STATES
OF AMERICA
WILL CONTINUE TO
REMEMBER THAT MANY
WHO TOILED HERE
FOUND THEIR FINAL
REST WHILE ENGAGED
IN THE BUILDING
OF THIS DAM

THEY DIED TO MAKE THE DESERT BLOOM

THE UNITED STATES
OF AMERICA
WILL CONTINUE TO
REMEMBER THE SERVICES
OF ALL WHO LABORED TO
CLOTHE WITH SUBSTANCE
THE PLANS OF THOSE WHO
FIRST VISIONED THE
BUILDING OF THIS DAM

paid to any free spending. Workers were housed in rows of tents, creating the fledgling town known as Boulder City where drinking and gambling were prohibited. Las Vegas was reserved for the weekend.

Working in harsh desert conditions, many lives were lost during completion of the dam. It was finally dedicated on 30 September 1935 by President Franklin D Roosevelt as millions tuned in by radio to hear him proclaim it a '20th-century marvel'. Then, as the dam held back the mighty Colorado, it created Lake Mead, America's largest man-made reservoir, named after Reclamation Commissioner Dr Elwood Mead. The lake can store 9.2 trillion US gallons of water, which is drawn into the dam by intake towers and flows through penstocks to the powerplant. The first generator was installed in 1936, followed by a further 16 to generate more than four billion kilowatt-hours of electricity per year.

Herbert Hoover, the 31st US President, became one of the greatest supporters of the project and in 1947 the Boulder Dam was officially renamed Hoover Dam in his honour. He believed that the dam should be self-financed through the sale of electricity and by this method the $165-million cost of the project was repaid.

As a National Historic Landmark, Hoover Dam is open to the public and it is visited by over one million people each year. Attendance can reach 4,000 in just one day.

Opposite: The Hoover Dam and Lake Mead beyond
Above: Tribute to dam workers

The Hoover Dam and Lake Mead

Hoover Dam and Lake Mead are two breathtaking sights located just a short drive away from Las Vegas. Both man-made creations, the Hoover Dam was constructed to harness the great Colorado River, while Lake Mead rose from the backed-up water heading south from the Rocky Mountains.

The Hoover Dam arch

Hoover Dam

Open all year round, you can drive or walk over the great arch of the Hoover Dam, which is located southeast of Las Vegas on the Nevada–Arizona border. It is forbidden to stop your car on the dam, situated on US Highway 93, but there are parking facilities at the Hoover Dam Visitor Center. The Discovery Tour of the dam is inexpensive and features a filmshow detailing its construction and an unforgettable tour inside the power plant. The busiest times to visit are during the summer months and spring break. Arrive early in the day to avoid the heat and the crowds.

Lake Mead

The largest man-made reservoir in the United States, Lake Mead offers an impressive 880km (550 miles) of shoreline and has a storage capacity of 3.5 billion cubic metres (9,299,792,116,392 US gallons!). In 1964 it was proclaimed as the first National Recreation Area, and it offers

Lake Mead offers several marinas and watersports activities

watersports including swimming, boating and fishing, sightseeing activities, lodging, camping and simply sunbathing. Diverse ecosystems from the Mohave Desert, the Great Basin and the Sonoran Deserts all intersect at Lake Mead, providing resources for wildlife education and conservation.

Approximately 40km (25 miles) from Las Vegas at its closest point, Lake Mead is open all year round and can easily be reached off the Boulder Highway on Route 93. Areas such as Las Vegas Bay, Lake Mead Marina and Boulder Beach feature restaurants, marinas, sporting activities and sightseeing cruises, particularly at Boulder Beach which is closer to the dam. There are also several islands such as Black Island or the Boulder Islands within the lake, which stretches far over the border into Arizona.

The Alan Bible Visitor Center is located off US Highway 93 near Boulder City and other visitor centres are situated at Overton Beach, Echo Bay, Callville Bay, Las Vegas Bay and Temple Bar in Arizona.

Around Lake Mead there are several lodging and camping facilities against a backdrop of ridges, mountains and desert over the crystal-blue waters of the lake.

Hoover Dam, US Route 93, Boulder City. Tel: (702) 494 2517. Visitor centre open daily (except for Thanksgiving and Christmas) 9am–5pm. Parking garage open 8am–5.45pm. Admission is inexpensive, but there is an added parking fee. Food and drink are not allowed on the tour but water bottles can be carried. The Hoover Dam Visitor Center and the Hoover Dam Discovery Tour are accessible for wheelchairs.

Lake Mead National Recreation Area, 601 Nevada Highway, Boulder City. Tel: (702) 293 8907/(702) 293 8990 (weekends). Lake Mead is open all year round, 24 hours a day. Visitor centre open daily (except Thanksgiving, Christmas and New Year's Day) 8.30am–4.30pm.

Power generators inside Hoover Dam

Desert landscape

Other excursions

While Las Vegas is the creation of the 20th century, located just a few miles outside the city are many national parks offering breathtaking geological formations and scenery. From imposing rock formations to the depths of the canyons, the area around Las Vegas offers a rich diversity of landscapes.

Mount Charleston

Located 56km (35 miles) northwest of Las Vegas in the Toiyabe National Forest, Mount Charleston rises to 3,632m (11,918ft). Visitors can enjoy horseriding, cycling and hiking, while winter activities include skiing, snowboarding and sleigh rides. There are hotels available all year round and camping facilities from May to September. The temperatures at Mount Charleston can be 20–30°F lower than in Las Vegas, so although it may be a welcome break from the heat, make sure you take adequate clothing. From Las Vegas, you can reach Mount Charleston from Kyle Canyon, State Highway 157, northwest of the city off Route 95.
Tel: (702) 873 8800, or ask at your hotel desk for travel information.

Red Rock Canyon

With its stunning rock formations, Red Rock Canyon is popular for anyone with a passion to explore. For those with an adventurous spirit there are cliffs, sheer drops and hidden crevices, along with a paved 21-km (13-mile) loop drive for those who want to take things a little easier. The scenery is outstanding,

thanks to the Keystone Thrust Fault which has thrust ancient grey rocks over the top of newer red sandstone. The red-blazoned rocks are complemented by sweeping sand dunes in an area which is also home to wild burros, bighorn sheep, feral horses and coyotes. Only 24km (15 miles) west of Las Vegas, the Red Rock Canyon Recreation Area can be reached from Charleston Boulevard, which meets State Highway 159 to the west of Las Vegas; the road then loops around the side of the canyon area to join the 160 back into the city.

Famed for its rock-climbing opportunities, other recreational activities available include cycling, climbing and hiking, while there

If you drive through the desert by car, you will see a few signs leading you to ghost towns such as Rhyolite, which is described as the Gateway to Death Valley. Located near to Beatty Nevada, 192km (120 miles) north of Las Vegas, Rhyolite includes ruins of the general store, banks, a school, railroad depot and a house made entirely from glass bottles.

are sites of geological and historical interest along with a museum and visitor centre.

Open: daily 6am–8pm in summer (closes at 5pm in winter).
Tel: (702) 363 1921, or ask at your hotel desk for travel information.

Death Valley

Located in western California, Death Valley National Park, at 85m (280ft) below sea level, is the lowest point in the Northern Hemisphere. This 250-km (155-mile) trench runs between the Amargosa mountain range on the east and the Panamint range to the west. The highest point in the range is Telescope Peak at 3,368m (11,049ft), only 24km (15 miles) from the lowest point of Badwater Basin salt pan.

Death Valley is 216km (135 miles) east of Las Vegas, and you can see many examples of the earth's diverse geological eras. Its harsh desert environment creates unique plant and animal species but the heat can be intense. Although the area seems too inhospitable for human life, archaeologists have found evidence of miners, prospectors and settlers, while Native Americans still reside in the area today. *Tel: (760) 786 3200.* *www.nps.gov/deva*

Death Valley

Valley of Fire State Park

Valley of Fire State Park

The Valley of Fire State Park is 88km (55 miles) northwest of Las Vegas on State Highway 176, off Interstate 15. Mysterious petroglyphs provide evidence of ancient Native American civilisations hidden within the beautiful canyon landscape with its red rock formations. The Valley of Fire State Park is close to Overton, home of the Lost City Museum, which provides a fascinating insight into the Anasazi, or ancient ones, who lived in the valley centuries ago.

The Nevada Park Service runs a visitor centre in the Valley of Fire State Park and tours are also available. The park is open to visitors all year round.

Bryce Canyon

With unique rock formations such as the Pink Cliffs, Silent City and the Cathedral, Bryce Canyon is a magnificent sight located 336km (210 miles) northeast of Las Vegas in southwestern Utah. It is open all year round. *Tel: (435) 834 5322. www.nps.gov/brca*

Mohave National Preserve

The Mohave National Preserve is a 0.64-million-hectare (1.6-million-acre) preserve which includes volcanic cinder cones, Joshua tree forests, sand dunes and mountains. Located 96km (60 miles) southwest of Las Vegas, the visitor centres are in Baker and Needles, California. *Tel: (760) 252 6100. www.nps.gov/moja*

Spring Mountain State Park

This ranch was once owned by billionaire Howard Hughes and was originally a resting point for travellers on the Mormon and Spanish trails. Located 48km (30 miles) west of Las Vegas, the park is open all year round and offers outdoor theatre and jazz concerts. *Tel: (775) 962 5102. www.parks.nv.gov/sv.htm*

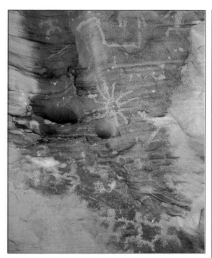

An ancient petroglyph in the Valley of Fire

LOS ANGELES

Certainly not a wonder of nature, but the city of Los Angeles, like Las Vegas, made its mark in the 20th century. By car you can reach Los Angeles in five to six hours and it is worthwhile taking a couple of days out to visit Disneyland and Universal Studios, or to see the stars on Hollywood Boulevard and the homes of the rich and famous in Beverly Hills. Plan your trip carefully, as the roads are known for their congestion and Los Angeles is a vast city to navigate.

Zion Canyon

Zion National Park is situated in Utah, at the junction of the Colorado Plateau, Great Basin and the Mohave Desert 253km (158 miles) north of Las Vegas on Interstate 15. Hebrew in origin, the name Zion describes the area as a place of sanctuary – and with its majestic rock formations, forest plateaus and vast deserts areas, the park certainly gives you the opportunity to see Mother Nature at her best. The Zion Canyon is formed by the Virgin River carving its way through the sandstone to create canyon walls up to 900m (3,000ft) high, while the river creates lush greenery along its flow. *Tel: (435) 772 3256. www.nps.gov/zion*

Zion National Park

Nevada is home to several Native American tribes, such as the Washo, Shoshone, Gosha and Paiute. The earliest known settlers were the Anasazi or 'Ancient ones', with the only clues to their existence being offered in rock etchings known as petroglyphs.

North Nevada is famed as cowboy territory, and references to the Wild West can be found throughout the state. In its early years as a tourist destination, Las Vegas housed a collection of western saloons and dude ranches, where guests could ride horses and play the part of a cowboy for a couple of weeks. The first Downtown establishments had wooden sawdust-covered floors, and the same western theme was carried on with the first buildings on the Strip. Starting with the railroads in the late 19th century, America was going through some great changes. In the 1930s and '40s, after the First World War and the hardships of the Great Depression, and in the midst of a new conflict, resorts such as El Rancho and the Last Frontier offered a last chance to hold on to the Old West.

Today, visitors to Nevada can still visit dude ranches. If you want to work a little harder, you can drive cattle and round up horses by staying on a working ranch, while adept horse riders can take part in exhilarating horse drives. Many side trips from Las Vegas take in cowboy ranches or Indian reservations, and they are often offered as part of coach and helicopter tours to the Grand Canyon.

Just 45 minutes from the Strip, Bonnie Springs Old Nevada was a frequent resting point for travellers on the old Spanish trail to California. Now, in this Wild West theme park, visitors can witness dramatic action that includes gunfights and hangings, in an old town that features a post office, blacksmith display, various old stores and the Boot Hill cemetery. This is a great attraction for children, who can also enjoy the petting zoo and rides.

There are several Native American reservations around the Las Vegas area. You can take part in a pow wow, a traditional get-together where tribes gather to exchange gifts, sell

food and crafts and hear the news. These festive meetings include tribal dances and rodeos, such as the Snow Mountain Pow Wow, which is held by the Las Vegas Colony, northwest of the city, on Memorial Day weekend in May.

Northeast of Las Vegas is the Moapa Indian Reservation, known for its duty-free tobacco and fireworks, although the latter are prohibited outside the reservation area, while the Fort Mohave reservation is just south of the Laughlin area.

East of Las Vegas on Interstate 15 is the Lost City Museum in Overton, with Anasazi artefacts and reconstructed pit dwellings. They lived in the Moapa Valley from the 1st to the 12th centuries, close to the Valley of Fire State Park where petroglyphs and stunning rock formations can be found.

Opposite: Wild West cowboys
Above (both): Bonnie Springs Old Nevada, originally built in 1843 on the old Spanish trail

Shopping

Leave plenty of room in your suitcase when you pack for Las Vegas. Within an 8-km (5-mile) radius of the Strip there are over 2.3 million sq m (25 million sq ft) of retail outlets, from hotel shops and designer malls to outlet villages. The international visitor spends an average of $252 on each trip to Las Vegas – and if you remove the men from that calculation that average is likely to double!

The Desert Passage

The main resorts all have shopping areas, such as Bally's Avenue Shoppes, Le Boulevard at Paris, Mandalay Bay Shops and Mandalay Place, Masquerade Village at the Rio, MGM Grand Avenue Shops, Monte Carlo Street of Dreams, New York–New York Shops, Street of Shops at the Mirage or the Tower Shops at Stratosphere. Some of the larger shopping malls offer restaurants, entertainment and free attractions. Away from the Strip there are many even larger shopping malls and outlet centres, the ideal place to buy designer goods at bargain prices.

Shopping centres on the Strip are usually open from around 10am until 10pm.

THE LAS VEGAS STRIP
Desert Passage

The Desert Passage features over 170 shops including Aveda, Steve Madden, Tommy Bahama, Z Gallerie and several restaurants.

Desert Passage on the Strip, with over 170 shops

Desert Passage, 3663 Las Vegas Blvd S.
www.desertpassage.com

The Forum Shops at Caesars

Known for its talking statues and beautiful interior landscaping, after a recent extension the Forum Shops feature over 63,000sq m (700,000sq ft) of retail stores that include Louis Vuitton, Escada, Gucci, Guess, Christian Dior, NikeTown, Polo/Ralph Lauren and Hugo Boss, as well as several restaurants including Wolfgang Puck's famed Spago and Planet Hollywood. Caesars is also home to the Appian Way, with 15 upmarket retailers, marble walkways, statues of Joe Louis and Michelangelo's David along with a Brahma shrine and the Palace temple. Shops include Cartier, Le Paradis, Cottura, Galerie Michelangelo, Piazza Del Mercato, Godiva Chocolatier, Bernini Couture, Carina and Paradiso.
Caesars Palace, 3570 Las Vegas Blvd S.
www.caesarspalace.com

The Fashion Show Mall

This multi-level mall in the centre of the Strip offers nearly 180,000sq m (2 million sq ft) of retail stores that include Neiman-Marcus, Saks Fifth Avenue, Bloomingdale's Home, Macy's, Dillard's, Robinsons-May and Nordstrom. An impressive new food hall has recently been added to the mall, with a balcony overlooking the strip.
3200 Las Vegas Blvd S. Adjacent to the New Frontier Hotel.

Grand Canal Shoppes at the Venetian

Surrounding the Grand Canal, featuring street entertainers and the beautiful St Mark's Square, this shopping centre has over 45,000sq m (500,000sq ft) of retail outlets that include Burberry, Bebe and Jimmy Choo. Like Caesars and Desert Passage, these are great areas for fashion shoppers.
Venetian Resort Hotel & Casino, 3355 Las Vegas Blvd S. www.venetian.com

Le Boulevard at Paris Las Vegas

Shop through Parisian streets featuring authentic French boutiques such as the wine merchants Le Cave, or find children's toys at Les Enfants, along with crystal and jewellery at La Boutique by Yokohama de Paris.
Paris Las Vegas, 3655 Las Vegas Blvd S. Located where Paris joins Bally's. www.parislasvegas.com

Via Bellagio

Within Bellagio's luxurious surroundings, this shopping promenade offers over 9,290sq m (100,000sq ft) of designer boutiques that include Chanel, Giorgio Armani, Prada, Tiffany & Co, Moschino, Yves Saint Laurent, Hermès and Gucci.
Bellagio, 3600 Las Vegas Blvd S. www.bellagio.com

OFF-STRIP SHOPPING
The Boulevard Mall

With 100,000sq m (1.13 million sq ft) of retail outlets, this is one of Nevada's largest shopping centres, with stores that include Footlocker, Gap, JC Penney, Sears, Dillard's and Macy's.
The Boulevard Mall, 3528 Maryland Parkway, Las Vegas. www.boulevardmall.com

The Fashion Show Mall on the Las Vegas Strip

Galleria at Sunset

This mall, 19km (12 miles) east of Las Vegas in Henderson, includes JC Penney, Robinsons-May, Dillard's, Cache, Champs Sports, Victoria's Secret and The Disney Store, along with a 600-seat food court.
1300 West Sunset Road, Henderson.
www.galleriaatsunset.com

The Meadows Mall

With two levels of shops and five courtyards, the Meadows Mall includes Dillard's, Macy's, JC Penney and Sears. The mall is located on US 95 Expressway, although it provides a trolley service from the Downtown Transportation Center.
4300 Meadows Lane, Las Vegas.
www.meadowsmall.com

OUTLET SHOPPING
Fashion Outlet Las Vegas

Located 56km (35 miles) south of the city in Primm on the Nevada–California

border, this outlet offers over 100 brand-name stores including DKNY, Calvin Klein, Kenneth Cole, Harley-Davidson, Bath & Body Works and Wilson's Leather. There are shuttles from the Las Vegas Strip from New York–New York and the MGM Grand.
32100 Las Vegas Blvd S, Primm.
www.fashionoutletlasvegas.com

Las Vegas Outlet Center
Frequent visitors will remember this as Belz Factory Outlet, just south of the Las Vegas Strip. With countless brand-name bargains at 20–70 per cent discount, stores include Saks Fifth Ave, Reebok, Levi's, the Greg Norman Collection and Fila. You can get a Citizens Area Transit (CAT) bus from the Las Vegas Strip to the centre, or it is a very short drive by taxi or car.
7400 Las Vegas Blvd S.

Las Vegas Premium Outlets
Over 40,000sq m (435,000sq ft) of stores in a new $80-million shopping centre

> **ONLY IN LAS VEGAS …**
>
> … can you find the **Bonanza Gift Shop**, located next to the Stratosphere, where you can buy every Vegas souvenir possible from personalised dice to mini slot machines. Gambling fanatics can purchase gaming memorabilia at the **Gamblers General Store**, Downtown on 800 South Main Street, or the **Casino Legends Hall of Fame** gift shop in the Tropicana. You can find the very best vintage clothing and all things retro at **The Attic**, located at 1018 South Main Street.

that includes over 100 designer names such as Armani Exchange, Dolce & Gabbana, Guess, Kenneth Cole, Lacoste, Polo Ralph Lauren Factory Store, St John, Tahari, Theory and Tommy Hilfiger Company Store. Savings range from 25 to 75 per cent.
875 South Grand Central Parkway,
Las Vegas.
www.premiumoutlets.com

The colourful exterior of Fashion Outlet Las Vegas

Entertainment

Never were you offered so much choice for entertainment. On stage, with production shows, comedy clubs, world-class celebrities and magicians, Las Vegas has it all. From the early lounge shows featuring legends like Louis Prima and Nat King Cole, the city has always presented high-profile celebrities, now adding Tom Jones, the Rolling Stones, Tony Bennett, Dwight Yoakam, Paul McCartney, Neil Diamond, Céline Dion and Elton John to its unrivalled listings.

Bellagio entrance

'O' at Bellagio

While you are in Las Vegas, do not miss acclaimed production shows such as *Mystère, KÀ, 'O'* and *Zumanity* by Cirque du Soleil and Dragone's *Le Rêve* at Wynn, while brand-new productions coming to Las Vegas include *Phantom of the Opera* at the Venetian and *Monty Python's Spamalot*. Interact with the players in dinner shows such as *Ba-Da-Bing, Tournament of the Kings* or *Tony 'n' Tina's Wedding* as the guest at their chaotic reception, complete with a drunken minister and pregnant bridesmaid. There are variety shows with a difference such as the glitzy *Jubilee*, which features the sinking of the *Titanic* every night, the great-value *Viva Las Vegas* at the Stratosphere, or *V – the Ultimate Variety Show*, which features some of the most unusual acts in the business.

Most production shows offer their own blend of comedy and entertainment, but the city is also home to several comedy clubs such as Improv at Harrah's, Riviera Comedy Club or The Comedy Stop at the Tropicana, a show that features three up-and-coming comedians on a bill that changes weekly. Rita Rudner is in residence in New York–New York, where she was voted Comedian of the Year, while the wacky Carrot Top is a frequent visitor to the Strip, along with award-winning headliners such as Ray Romano, Jackie Mason or Jerry Seinfeld who often performs at Caesars Palace. The Rio offers family shows with *Ronn Lucas* and *The Scintas*, featuring comedy, music and impressions, and the Flamingo presents *The Second City*, a 40-year-old institution of comedy and improvisation.

Known as Sin City, Las Vegas is also renowned for adult shows such as *Crazy Girls*, *La Femme*, *Bite* or *Fantasy*. You can see uncensored hypnotists such as Anthony Cools at Paris, who claims that you should leave all inhibitions at home, and has audiences returning night after

night in case they miss out on more outrageous antics.

In a city filled with tribute acts you can see shows dedicated to Elvis Presley and the Beatles, or sip cocktails with the Rat Pack at the Greek Isles in *The Tribute to Frank, Sammy, Joey and Dean*. Only in Las Vegas could you see Elvis Presley sharing a stage with Britney Spears and Christina Aguilera in *American Superstars* at the Stratosphere, while *An Evening At La Cage* at the Riviera features Frank Marino as Joan Rivers, joining a cast of A-list divas such as Madonna, Cher and Whitney Houston.

In short, there are more shows and opportunities for entertainment than you could fit into a single visit to Las Vegas. *See the guide to must-see productions on pp128–33, and suggestions for free entertainment on pp134–5.*

Family fun with the *Tournament of Kings* at Excalibur

The Rat Pack

In January 1960, the Rat Pack held court at the Sands Hotel. Frank Sinatra, Dean Martin, Sammy Davis Jr, Peter Lawford and Joey Bishop were in Las Vegas to film the classic casino heist *Ocean's Eleven* and every evening, after production wrapped, they took to the stage at the Copa Room.

Hotel rooms were booked throughout the city, as people clambered for the chance to see Frank and his buddies on stage. On some nights, only one or two would appear, but on lucky occasions, audiences were entertained by the whole pack.

They were the ultimate Kings of Cool, and breezed through filming, refusing to commit more than a single take, as they ad-libbed through each scene with drinks in hand. The same happened on stage. Dean Martin would drift into the spotlight 'direct from the bar', as he was introduced, and with drink in one hand, cigarette in the other, he would croon effortlessly through *Volare* or *That's Amore*. Dean had been performing in Las Vegas since he first partnered Jerry Lewis in the '40s, and was followed on stage at the Sands by another Vegas regular, Sammy Davis Jr, who first played the city when he was 19. As a performer, Sammy burst with energy and his powerhouse vocals and frantic tap routines were exhausting just to witness, as Frank, Dean and the rest of the pack just pulled up a bar stool on stage and watched him. As for the chairman of the board, Frank Sinatra was also a huge name in Las Vegas. He made his first appearance at the Desert Inn in 1941 and remained a headliner in the city for over 40 years.

'This is Frank's world,' Dean would quip. 'We just live in it.'

The Rat Pack Summit was named in jest after the Paris Summit, which gathered Dwight D Eisenhower, then the US President, with French and Soviet leaders. Frank also had his own political aspirations and publicly backed John F Kennedy's campaign for the White House, inviting Kennedy's brother-in-law Peter Lawford into his fold. Writer-comedian Joey Bishop led the humour for the pack, but collectively their antics brought the house to hysterics. As a mini-bar was wheeled on stage, they sipped Martinis and entertained their celebrity-filled audiences until the early hours, leaving a permanent marker in entertainment history.

Backstage, the party was just beginning.

Share a toast with Frank and his buddies in one of the Rat Pack tribute shows in Las Vegas. These highly acclaimed productions, complete with swingin' big bands, have taken residence at various Vegas nightspots over the years, with recent shows taking place at the Greek Isles. Check the printed show guides or your hotel box office to find the latest venue.

Opposite: The Venetian was built on the site of the Sands Hotel
Above: The Rat Pack is synonymous with Las Vegas

Showtime on the Strip

Las Vegas offers the very best in entertainment and the demand for many of its world-class production shows means that you may have to book tickets as soon as you have confirmed your travel arrangements. However, while you are in Vegas, the choice is still endless and many shows offer discounts or special offers which you can find in the local guides located in most hotels.

Mirage marquee

Starting prices for shows, per adult:

★	Under $25
★★	$25–$50
★★★	$51–$100
★★★★	Over $100

Production shows

An Evening at La Cage★★

Frank Marino, the self-proclaimed Queen of the Las Vegas Strip, portrays Joan Rivers to lead a hilarious Vegas-style version of this famous Parisian cabaret.

The Riviera Hotel & Casino, 2901 Las Vegas Blvd S. Shows: daily 7.30pm. No show Tue.

Blue Man Group★★★

The stars of this show are three bright-blue bald men who have won audiences over across the globe. If your curiosity wins out, you will be rewarded by an outrageous performance, but beware, you will be given a protective poncho if you sit too near the front!

Venetian Resort Hotel & Casino, 3355 Las Vegas Blvd S. Shows: daily 7pm, Sat 7pm & 10pm.

Danny Gans: The Man of Many Voices★★★★

Danny Gans can perform over 300 impersonations, where he not only imitates celebrity voices but takes on their personalities too. His celebrated family show is presented in a lavish $15-million theatre which was custom-built for the entertainer.

The Mirage, 3400 Las Vegas Blvd S. Tel: (702) 792 7777. Shows: daily 8pm. No show Mon & Fri.

Folies Bergère★★

This variety act is the longest-running showgirl revue in Las Vegas. The first of their two nightly performances in the Tiffany Theater, the 7.30pm show, sees the dancers fully clothed.

See pp56–7 for details on this and similar shows.

The Tropicana, 3801 Las Vegas Blvd S. Tel: (702) 739 2222. Shows: 7.30pm & 10pm, Tue & Fri 8.30pm.

Hairspray★★★

Set in Baltimore in the 1960s and winner of eight Tony Awards, this hilarious musical follows the story of big-haired, big-teen Tracy Turnblad and her quest to dance her way onto TV's most popular dance show.

Luxor Hotel & Casino, 3900 Las Vegas Blvd S. Tel: (702) 262 4000.
Shows: 7pm Mon & Fri, 7pm and 10pm Tue, Thur, Sat & Sun.

Blue Man Group at the Venetian

Jubilee★★★

With million-dollar sets and costumes by Emmy Award-winning designer Bob Mackie, *Jubilee* is voted as the best showgirl revue in Las Vegas. This must-see spectacular includes singers, dancer acrobats and a dramatic scene featuring the sinking of the *Titanic*. *Bally's Las Vegas, 3645 Las Vegas Blvd S. Tel: (702) 739 4111. Shows: daily 7.30pm & 10.30pm. No show Fri. All-access backstage tickets can also be purchased.*

KÀ★★★★

Described as Cirque du Soleil's most ambitious production, *KÀ* presents the tale of two Imperial twins and their epic journey through life. A cast of over 80 performers combine martial arts, acrobatics, puppetry, interactive video projections and pyrotechnics to create an exciting, awe-inspiring performance. *MGM Grand Hotel and Casino, 3799 Las Vegas Blvd S. Tel: (702) 891 1111. Shows: 7.30pm & 10.30pm Tue–Sat.*

Lance Burton, Master Magician★★★

This acclaimed illusionist is a Las Vegas favourite. In this family show, Burton makes a whole convertible disappear and often enlists the audience to help with his illusions. *The Monte Carlo Resort & Casino, 3770 Las Vegas Blvd S. Tel: (702) 730 7777. Shows: Tue & Sat 7pm & 10pm; Wed, Thur & Fri 7pm only.*

Legends in Concert★

The original Las Vegas tribute show, running for over 20 years with an ever-changing list of stars that includes Elvis, Ricky Martin, Prince and Madonna.

Check local guides for more discounts and promotions for this popular show. *Imperial Palace Hotel & Casino, 3535 Las Vegas Blvd S. Tel: (702) 731 3311. Shows: daily 7.30pm & 10.30pm. No show Sun.*

Le Rêve: A Small Collection of Imperfect Dreams★★★

With every seat at centre stage, *Le Rêve* features a cast of artists and athletes from around the world, performing outstanding acrobatic feats. Characters rise, fall and are created from fire, rain or the infinite depths of *Le Rêve's* aquatic stage. *Wynn Las Vegas, 3131 Las Vegas Blvd S. Tel: (702) 770 7000. Shows: Sat–Wed 7.30pm & 10.30pm. No show Thur & Fri.*

Magic of Rick Thomas★

Featuring rare white tigers, which appear and disappear before your eyes, this is a great value-for-money family show that has been credited as the most successful daytime show of its kind. *Stardust Resort and Casino, 3000 Las Vegas Blvd S. Tel: (702) 732 6111. Shows: daily 2pm & 4pm. No show Wed.*

Mamma Mia!★★★

Singing and dancing in the aisles is guaranteed, as 22 of ABBA's greatest hits accompany the uplifting tale of bride-to-be Sophie on her emotional, and sometimes chaotic, journey to discover the identity of her real father. *Mandalay Bay, 3950 Las Vegas Blvd S. Tel: (702) 632 7777. Shows: Sun–Thur 7.30pm; Sat 6pm & 10pm.*

A Musical Tribute To Liberace★

This short, but great-value, show could

not be better placed than amongst the pomp and splendour of the Liberace Museum. Playing Liberace's legendary rhinestone piano, Wes Winters invites full audience participation in celebrating the sparkling career of Mr Showmanship.

Liberace Museum, 1775 E. Tropicana Ave. Tel: (702) 798 5595. Shows: Wed, Thur & Sat 1pm.

Mystère **by Cirque du Soleil**★★★

Playing in Las Vegas for over 10 years, *Mystère* unravels the human potential with a cast of over 72 gymnasts, acrobats, clowns, dancers, singers and musicians from this world-famous production company.
TI, 3300 Las Vegas Blvd S. Tel: (702) 796 9999. Shows: Wed–Sat 7.30pm & 10.30pm; Sun 4.30pm & 7.30pm. No show Mon & Tue.

'O' by Cirque du Soleil★★★

With 81 artists performing in, around, over and under a 1.5-million-gallon pool of water, 'O' is a breathtaking presentation of theatre through the ages.
Bellagio, 3600 Las Vegas Blvd S. Tel: (702) 693 7111. Shows: Wed–Sun 7.30pm & 10.30pm.

'O' by Cirque du Soleil

The Grand Garden Arena at MGM Grand

Penn & Teller★★

With the tagline 'if you're lucky, nobody gets injured', the bad boys of magic have earned critical acclaim across the globe for bringing a new dynamic to this old craft. *Rio All-Suite Hotel & Casino, 3700 West Flamingo Road. Tel: (702) 777 7777. Shows: Wed–Sun 9pm. No show Mon & Tue.*

Tony 'n' Tina's Wedding★★★

With a ticket price that includes dinner, tips and a champagne toast, join Tony and Tina as a guest at their tacky wedding reception, as the other guests and the family cause havoc. You can even pose for the wedding photographer in a show which brings audience participation to a new level. *Rio All-Suite Hotel & Casino, 3700 West Flamingo Road. Tel: (702) 777 7777. Shows: daily 7pm. VIP tickets are also available.*

Tournament of Kings★★

Forget the cutlery and your table manners in this riotous medieval joust. With over 100 performers, this is a popular show for all the family. *Excalibur Hotel & Casino, 3850 Las Vegas Blvd S. Tel: (702) 597 7777. Shows: daily 6pm & 8.30pm.*

Tribute to Frank, Sammy, Joey and Dean★★

There have been several Rat Pack tribute shows in Las Vegas, including this latest show at the Greek Isles, where Frank Sinatra, Dean Martin, Sammy Davis Jr and comedian Joey Bishop take you back to their swinging era of Las Vegas in the '60s. A hilarious show with a live big band.

The Greek Isles Hotel & Casino, 305 Convention Center Drive.
Tel: (702) 734 0711. Shows: Sat–Thur 8.15pm. A dinner show is also available, starting at 6pm.

Headliners

There are always headliners on the Strip. Some are in residence, and stars including Tony Bennett, Jerry Seinfeld, Neil Diamond and Tom Jones have recently appeared along with the many entertainers who include the city on their tours. At the time of writing, ongoing headliners include the following:

Céline Dion in *A New Day*★★★★

This acclaimed production presents a cast of 58 performers, state-of-the-art technology and lighting, 3D screen graphics and the legendary Céline in person. Stunning European sets extend from the performance area to house the audience in the 4,000-seat colosseum at Caesars Palace.

Caesars Palace, 3570 Las Vegas Blvd S.
Tel: (702) 731 7110. www.celinedion.com.
Shows: Wed–Sun 8.30pm.

Elton John: The Red Piano★★★★

Winning several awards since opening in 2004, the show features Elton John's vivid red piano set before the Colosseum's huge LED screen, which projects a rich, and sometimes provocative, imagery of Hollywood and Las Vegas icons, to accompany hits ranging from *Rocket Man* to *Candle In The Wind*.

Caesars Palace, 3570 Las Vegas Blvd S.
Tel: (702) 731 7110.
Shows: daily 7.30pm, unless shows are scheduled for Céline Dion. No show Mon & Thur.

Barry Manilow in Manilow: Music and Passion★★★

After his last tour sold out to over 250,000 fans, Barry Manilow was enticed to Las Vegas for this long-running engagement featuring classic pop songs from *Copacabana* to *Bermuda Triangle*, and famed ballads such as *I Write The Songs*. One not to miss.

Las Vegas Hilton, 3000 Paradise Road.
Tel: (702) 732 5111. Shows: Wed–Fri 9pm; Sat 7.30pm & 10pm.

Entertainment venues

For your one chance to see your favourite entertainers on tour, make sure you check listings for venues such as the MGM Grand Arena, which has recently hosted the Rolling Stones, Bon Jovi, Paul McCartney and the Billboard Music Awards. The House of Blues at Mandalay Bay always has a packed entertainment schedule and has featured Willie Nelson, CMT's Most Wanted Live Tour and Lisa Marie Presley, while the Joint at the Hard Rock Hotel has showcased acts such as David Bowie, KD Lang and Alanis Morissette.

Free entertainment

Just walking along the Strip, visiting the luxury resorts or people-watching in the casinos can provide hours of free entertainment, in addition to a multitude of free museums, wildlife attractions, stage shows and neon spectaculars, which seem almost too numerous to list here.

MGM Grand Lion Habitat

Azure
This choreographed underwater show features mermaids and mermen among over 4,000 tropical fish in the Silverton's new 117,000-gallon aquarium.
Silverton Hotel and Casino. 3333 Blue Diamond Road. Tel: (702) 363 7777. Shows: Wed & Thur 5pm & 10pm, Fri 5pm, Sat 2pm & 10pm, Sun 1pm & 7pm. No show Mon & Tue.

Bonnie & Clyde Exhibit
See newspaper reports on the couple, an intricate necklace made by Clyde while in prison, and their famous getaway car.
Primm Valley Resort, 31900 Las Vegas Blvd S. Interstate 15 south on the California border. Tel: (702) 386 7867. Open: 24 hours.

CBS Television City Research Center
Register for free tickets then watch the latest new television pilots and offer your own opinion on their future in television.
Located at the MGM Grand, 3799 Las Vegas Blvd S. Tel: (702) 891 5776. Open: daily 10am–10pm.

Performers in Excalibur

FREE ATTRACTIONS YOU MUST NOT MISS IN LAS VEGAS

The Fremont Street Experience (*see pp88–9*)

The Fountains at Bellagio (*see pp60–61 & 63*)

MGM Grand Lion Habitat (*see p136*)

The Mirage Volcano (*see p63*)

The Neon Museum (*see pp90–91 & 92–3*)

The Sirens of TI (*see p63*)

The Talking Statues at Caesars (*see pp52–3*)

Masquerade Show in the Sky
Floats are suspended above the crowd as the Rio presents its own Mardi Gras Carnival in the Masquerade Village.
Rio All-Suite Hotel & Casino. 3700 West Flamingo Road. Tel: (702) 777 7777. Shows: daily 3pm, 4pm, 5pm, 6.30pm, 7.30pm, 8.30pm & 9.30pm.

Other similar shows include the aerial display **Airplay** at the Tropicana and the Wild West **Sunset Stampede** in Sam's Town.

Nevada Test Site
Visit this fascinating museum detailing the history of the atomic bomb and nuclear testing in the Las Vegas area. The history centre is open daily but you must book in advance to visit the actual test site.
Nevada Test Site History Center, Losee Road and Energy Way, North Las Vegas.

Tel: (702) 295 1198. Open: Mon–Fri midday–4pm. To visit the test site call (702) 295 0945.

Penske Wynn Ferrari Maserati
Some of the rarest and most expensive luxury cars are on display in this 9,300-sq m (100,000-sq ft) showroom. Many price tags are in excess of $700,000, including Steve Wynn's $1.4-million Enzo Ferrari.
Wynn Las Vegas, 3131 Las Vegas Blvd S. Tel: (702) 770 2000.
Open: Mon–Sat 10am–9pm.

The World's Largest Permanent Circus
Live circus acts every 30 minutes, from trapeze artists and acrobats to tightrope walkers.
Circus Circus Hotel & Casino, 2880 Las Vegas Blvd S. Tel: (702) 734 0410. Shows: daily 11am–midnight.

Masquerade Show in the Sky at the Rio

Wildlife

The city of Las Vegas is home to several wildlife attractions, supported by acclaimed animal trainers and conservationists who have devoted their lives to preserving endangered species. Many of these attractions are located on the Strip and are free to the public, who can observe these rare animals in several unique environments.

A rare white tiger

Price guide:
★   Under $10
★★   Over $10

Flamingo Wildlife Habitat

Over 300 birds and animals in a tropical setting with waterfalls and lagoons right in the centre of the Strip. Over 30 species of birds live in natural environments, including African penguins, swans, ducks and the hotel's stunning mascot, the Chilean flamingo.
Flamingo Las Vegas, 3555 Las Vegas Blvd S. Tel: (702) 733 3111. Open: 24 hours. Admission: free.

MGM Grand Lion Habitat

The MGM Grand would not be complete without the company's trademark, or Leo the lion as moviegoers know him, so the hotel presents its own pride of lions. Watch these magnificent creatures interact with their trainers and study them up close as they laze above a walk-through tunnel.
MGM Grand, 3799 Las Vegas Blvd S. Tel: (702) 891 1111. Open: daily 11am–10pm, closed 3.45–4.20pm. Admission: free.

The Secret Garden of Siegfried & Roy

White tigers, elephants and other animals from Siegfried and Roy's collection can be viewed in this natural environment in the centre of the Strip. The Mirage is also home to the **Dolphin Habitat** where Atlantic bottlenose dolphins enjoy an environment that offers a coral reef and 9.5 million litres (2.5 million gallons) of swimming space.
The Mirage, 3400 Las Vegas Blvd S. Tel: (702) 791 7111. The Secret Garden of Siegfried & Roy and the Dolphin Habitat are open weekdays 11am–5.30pm and weekends 10am–5.30pm. Admission: adults★★, children 4–12★★, under 3 free.

Shark Reef

See dangerous reptiles, man-eating sharks and many varieties of fish as they soar over you in reef tunnels or bask around a sunken pirate ship. There is also a touch pool where you can touch stingrays and small sharks.
Mandalay Bay Resort & Casino, 3950 Las Vegas Blvd S. Tel: (702) 632 7777. Open: daily 11am–11pm. Admission: adults★★ children★ under 4 free (see pp50–51).

Silverton Hotel Aquarium

The new 117,000-gallon artificial reef and aquarium in the Silverton Casino features stingrays, sharks and 4,000 tropical fish from across the globe. There are several aquariums and wildlife exhibits throughout this hotel, including the hypnotic jellyfish aquariums in the Mermaid Lounge.

Silverton Hotel & Casino, 3333 Blue Diamond Rd. Tel: (702) 263 7777. Casino open 24 hours. The Mermaid Lounge is open weekdays 11am–2am, weekends 24hrs. Admission: free. Under 21s are not permitted in this bar.

South Nevada Zoological-Botanical Park

This Las Vegas zoo offers 150 plant and animal species, including apes, chimpanzees, wallabies and reptiles. The park also offers Desert Ecotours.

1775 North Rancho Drive. Tel: (702) 647 4685. Open: daily 9am–5pm. Admission★.

White Tiger Habitat

Siegfried and Roy have a ranch and jungle compound for these rare cats outside the city, but here you can view them in their Las Vegas residence.

The Mirage, 3400 Las Vegas Blvd S. Tel: (702) 791 7111. Open: daily 10.30am–10pm. Admission: free.

The observation tunnel at the MGM Grand Lion Habitat

Liberace: Mr Showmanship

Museums

Las Vegas offers a unique collection of museums on diverse subjects ranging from its Native American ancestry to show business and gambling. In keeping with most city attractions, most of the museums are open daily and for longer hours than you would expect in other cities.

Price guide:
★   Under $5
★★ $5–$10
★★★   Over $10

The Auto Collections

Over 350 vehicles are displayed, with attractions that include Elvis Presley's 1976 El Dorado and Sammy Davis Jr's Stutz Bearcat. Antiques, classics and speciality vehicles are also available for trade.

Imperial Palace Hotel & Casino, 3535 Las Vegas Blvd S. Tel: (702) 794 3174. www.autocollections.com. Open: daily 9.30am–11.30pm. Admission: adults★★ children★.

Clark County Heritage Museum

Following the history of southern Nevada from prehistoric times to the present day. A good museum highlighting how the area around Las Vegas evolved.
1830 South Boulder Highway, Henderson. Tel: (702) 455 7955. www.co.clark.nv.us. Open: daily 9am–4.30pm. Admission★.

Las Vegas Historic Museum

With one of the largest displays of casino memorabilia, this museum details the history of over 700 casinos, 550 of which no longer exist.
Tropicana Resort & Casino, 6801 Las Vegas Blvd S. Tel: (702) 739 2222. Open: daily 9am–9pm. Admission: adults★★ (no admission for under-18s).

Madame Tussaud's Celebrity Encounter at the Venetian

Las Vegas Natural History Museum

A non-profit-making organisation that presents dinosaur displays, fossils, marine life, Nevada wildlife, world wildlife and an Africa exhibit.
900 Las Vegas Blvd N. Tel: (702) 384 3466.
Open: daily 9am–4pm. Admission: adults★★ children★.

Liberace Museum

One of the most popular museums in Las Vegas, with dazzling costumes, pianos, cars and antiques from the most glittering of showmen.
1775 East Tropicana Ave. Tel: (702) 798 5595. www.liberace.org. Open: Mon–Sat noon–4pm, Sun 1–5pm. Admission★★★.

Lost Vegas Gambling Museum

Tracing the history of gambling in Las Vegas, this fascinating museum features casino artefacts such as gaming chips, matchbooks, playing cards and slot machines. It also has exhibits on visionaries such as Ben Siegel and Howard Hughes, as well as celebrities including Elvis, Liberace and the Rat Pack.
450 Fremont St. Tel: (702) 385 1883.
Open: daily 10am–8pm. Admission★.

Madame Tussaud's Celebrity Encounter

See over 100 stars in this interactive attraction, which includes world leaders and celebrities such as Jon Bon Jovi, Frank Sinatra, Elvis and Tiger Woods.
The Venetian, 3355 Las Vegas Blvd S. Tel: (702) 862 7800. www.mtvegas.com.
Open: daily 10am–10pm. Admission★★★.

Titanic: The Artifacts Exhibition

With over 300 artifacts discovered on the *Titanic*, this exhibit also includes the personal possessions of its passengers and crew, a 15-ton hull section and recreations that include a first-class cabin and the ship's mighty boiler room.
The Tropicana, 3801 Las Vegas Blvd S. Tel: (702) 739 2222.
Open: daily 10am–10pm, last admission 9pm. Admission★★★.

The Tomb & Museum of King Tutankhamun

With authentic reproductions of this legendary archaeological find, created with 3,300-year-old techniques to exact specifications.
Luxor, 3900 Las Vegas Blvd S. Tel: (702) 262 4000. Open: daily 9am–11.00pm. Admission★★.

Inside the magnificent Luxor pyramid

Art galleries

Las Vegas has always offered a wealth of creative outlets and art galleries, but when developer and art collector Steve Wynn opened the Bellagio Gallery of Fine Art in 1998, the city was suddenly recognised as a centre for the visual arts where you could view revered masterpieces and see the very best contemporary work from local, national and international artists.

The Guggenheim displays treasures from the Hermitage in St Petersburg

Art Encounter

Close to the Strip on Spring Mountain Road, which crosses Las Vegas Boulevard at TI, this is Nevada's largest fine-art gallery and features over 100 originals from local and national artists.
3979 Spring Mountain Road.
Tel: (702) 227 0220.
www.artencounter.com. Open: Tue–Fri 10am–6pm, Sat & Mon midday–5pm.

Bellagio Gallery of Fine Art

This gallery presents museum-calibre exhibitions from many prestigious international collections. Recent displays have included the Impressionist landscape from Corot to Van Gogh and *Andy Warhol: The Celebrity Portraits* featuring three decades of celebrity pictures including Jacqueline Kennedy, Elizabeth Taylor, Dennis Hopper, Sylvester Stallone and Michael Jackson. The Bellagio Gallery of Fine Art is dedicated to providing a cultural destination for visitors of all backgrounds and interests.
See p76.
Bellagio, 3600 Las Vegas Blvd S.
Tel: (702) 693 7871.
Open: daily 9am–10pm.

Collectors Fine Art

Located in Montelago Village at the picturesque Lake Las Vegas, this gallery features original artwork, limited edition prints, sculptures and hand-blown glass from internationally renowned artists as well as special exhibitions.
30 Via Brianza St, Suite 120, Henderson.
Tel: (702) 558 5078. Open: daily 10am–8pm.

Donna Beam Fine Art Gallery

Exhibits from all media, from national, international and local artists, this gallery is located in the University of Las Vegas. It also offers travelling exhibits.
4505 South Maryland Parkway.
Tel: (702) 895 3893. Open: Mon–Fri 9am–5pm, Sat 10am–2pm.

Guggenheim Hermitage Museum

A joint venture between the State Hermitage Museum in St Petersburg, Russia and New York's Solomon R Guggenheim Foundation, this celebrated museum first opened in 2001. Recent collections have included *Russia! The Majesty of the Tsars: Treasures from the Kremlin Museum. See pp76–7.*

The Venetian, 3355 Las Vegas Blvd S.
Tel: (702) 414 2440.
www.guggenheimlasvegas.org. Open: daily
9.30am–8.30pm.

Las Vegas Art Museum

Approximately 16km (10 miles) from
the Strip, the Las Vegas Art Museum is
the result of an arts project that started
in the 1950s, and it has grown into a
busy attraction which welcomes over
60,000 visitors each year. Affiliated to
the Smithsonian Institution, it features
touring exhibitions and works of art
from masters and recently added a

fascinating centenary exhibit.
9600 West Sahara Ave.
Tel: (702) 360 8000. Open: Tue–Sat
10am–5pm, Sun 1–5pm.

The Wynn Collection

Steve and Elaine Wynn's personal
and priceless collection of fine art.
Exhibits include masterworks by
Rembrandt, Renoir, Matisse and
Le Rêve by Picasso – an inspiration
for Wynn's luxurious new resort.
Wynn Las Vegas, 3131 Las Vegas Blvd S.
Tel: (702) 770 3599.
Open: Sun–Thur 10am–11pm.

The Las Vegas Art Museum attracts over 60,000 visitors each year

Theme parks and thrill rides

Las Vegas is the perfect city for adrenalin addicts and features some of the tallest and fastest rides in the world. Other attractions in this category give you the opportunity to relax and take in some of the magnificent sights on the Strip. *See also pp46–7.*

Marquee at Primm

Price guide:
★   Under $5
★★ $5–$10
★★★   Over $10

Adventuredome Theme Park

This indoor theme park features rides for all ages, but for thrill seekers try the double-loop, double-corkscrew coaster, the *Canyon Blaster*, the largest indoor rollercoaster in the world, along with the unpredictable ride *Chaos* with its three ranges of motion and the *Inverter*, with its constant G force, 360° flips and turns. A new ride in the *Adventuredome*, the *Sling Shot*, propels passengers up a 30-m (100-ft) tower at a terrifying 4G acceleration and finally, if you want a soaking before going out into the sun, try the *Rim Runner*, a log ride featuring an 18-m (60-ft) drop over a waterfall.
Circus Circus Hotel & Casino, 2880 Las Vegas Blvd S. Tel: (702) 794 3939. Open: Mon–Thur 10am–6pm, Fri–Sat 10am–midnight, Sun 10am–8pm. Riders must be 1.2m (4ft) or taller to ride the Canyon Blaster, Chaos, Sling Shot, Rim Runner and Inverter. Admission: free; rides★ premium rides★★ day pass★★★.

Buffalo Bill's Wild West Theme Park

Located 56km (35 miles) outside Las Vegas on the California–Nevada Border at Primm, Buffalo Bill's is home to the *Desperado* rollercoaster, with its terrifying 69-m (225-foot) drop, and the *Turbo Drop*, which plummets riders 52m (170ft) downwards at 72kph (45mph) to experience negative G force. Thrill seekers can also enjoy the programmable *MaxFlight Cybercoaster* and the *Adventure Canyon Log Flume* among other rides.
Primm, Interstate 15 South. Tel: (702) 382 1212. Open: Mon–Thur midday–6pm, Fri 11am–midnight, Sat 10am–midnight, Sun 10am–7pm. Riders must be at least 1.2m (4ft) for thrill rides. Prices★/★★.

Eiffel Tower Experience

Get a panoramic view of the city 100 storeys above the centre of the Strip.
Paris Las Vegas, 3655 Las Vegas Blvd S. Tel: (702) 946 7000. Open: daily 10am–1am. Admission★★ Fri–Sun★★★.

Flyaway Indoor Skydiving

Try the sport of bodyflight, and experience the sensation of skydiving indoors! Freefall into a wind tunnel supported by a column of air rushing at speeds of up to 192kph (120mph). *200 Convention Center Drive. Tel: (702) 731 4768. Open: 10am–6pm. Flights and coaching packages★★★.*

Gondola rides

After walking and shopping for hours in the Venetian, relax on the Grand Canal, while a singing gondolier serenades you. *Venetian, 3355 Las Vegas Blvd S. Tel: (702) 414 1000. Open: daily 10am–11pm, Fri & Sat 10am–11.45pm. Prices: adults★★★ under 12s★★.*

The NASCAR Café

Located at the Sahara, the NASCAR Café includes the *Las Vegas Cyber Speedway* and *Speed: the Ride*. With Speedway cars seven-eighths the size of actual race cars and mounted on hydraulic bases, experience authentic braking responses, torque and suspension on the *Las Vegas Cyber Speedway*, the ultimate driving experience. *Speed: the Ride* is one of the first linear-induction-motor rollercoasters in the western United States, racing from 56–112kph (35–70mph) in under two seconds. This heart-pounding ride runs underground and 69m (224ft) in the air and also races backwards. *Sahara Hotel & Casino, 2535 Las Vegas Blvd S. Tel: (702) 737 2111. Speed The Ride open: Sun–Thur 11am–midnight, Fri & Sat 11am–1am. The Las Vegas Cyber Speedway open: Sun–Thur 10am–midnight, Fri & Sat 10am–1am. Price★★★ per ride. Passes for both rides are available. Height restrictions apply.*

The NASCAR Café at the Sahara

The Manhattan Express winds around New York–New York

Manhattan Express

Reaching a height of 62m (203ft) and dropping 44m (144ft), this rollercoaster races around the exterior of New York–New York at 107kph (67mph) and includes the breathtaking heart line twist in front of the building.

New York–New York Hotel & Casino, 3790 Las Vegas Blvd S.
Tel: (702) 740 6969. Open: daily 11am–11pm. Riders must be 1.07m (3ft 6in) or taller. Admission★★★.

Merlin's Magic Motion Machine film ride

One of the best-value thrill rides on the Strip. Save the planet in *Comet Impact* and encounter live prehistoric creatures in *Dino Island*.

Excalibur Hotel & Casino, 3850 Las Vegas Blvd S. Tel: (702) 597 7777. Open: daily 10am–11pm. Admission★.

Pharaoh's Pavilion

Featuring *IMAX Ridefilm* presentations, plus the seven-storey *IMAX 3D Theater*, with wrap-around digital surround sound. The shows change frequently and have included Hollywood blockbusters and 3D presentations such as *Sharks 3D, Wild Safari, Mystery of the Nile, Magnificent Desolation: Walking on the Moon 3D* and *Fighter Pilot*. The *Games of the Gods Arcade* and the *Tomb and*

Museum of King Tutankhamun are also found in the Pavilion, along with the Atrium showroom which presents *Pirates 4D*, a hilarious comedy starring Leslie Neilson, which combines 3D visuals with special effects and interactive seats.

Luxor Hotel & Casino, 3900 Las Vegas Blvd S. Tel: (702) 262 4555.

Open: daily 9am–11pm. You must be at least 1.07m (3ft 6in) for the motion rides. Prices★★/★★★. Inclusive ride passes can also be purchased.

Star Trek: The Experience

Featuring the largest selection of *Star Trek* merchandise in the universe, Trekkies can also visit the *History Of The Future Museum, Star Trek The Experience – Secrets Unveiled* or confront Starfleet enemies in *Klingon Encounter* and *Borg Invasion 4D*.

Las Vegas Hilton, 3000 Paradise Rd. Tel: (702) 732 5111.

Open: Sun–Thur 11am–10pm, Fri & Sat 11am–11pm. Admission★★★.

Stratosphere Tower & Strat-o-Fair

On top of the tallest building west of the Mississippi are the four tallest thrill rides in the world. The *Big Shot* fires riders 48m (160ft) upwards from the top of the space needle. *Insanity – The Ride* spins riders face down over Vegas and *X Scream* propels them 8m (27ft) over the edge of the tower.

Stratosphere Tower Hotel & Casino, 2000 Las Vegas Blvd S. Tel: (702) 380 7777.

Open: daily 10am– 1am, Fri & Sat until 2am. Admission: tower only★ with passes for rides★★★. Height restrictions apply.

Inside the Adventuredome Theme Park at Circus Circus

Light at Bellagio

Nightclubs

The first nightclub on the Strip was the Pair-O-Dice Club, which was later known as the 91 Club and owned by Police Captain Guy McAfee – who is also credited for naming the Los Angeles highway 'the Strip'. Today there is a huge variety of nightlife to choose from, with lounge bars, hotel bars and nightclubs that open until dawn.

Price guide:
★　　　Under $10
★★　　$10–$15
★★★　$16–$20
★★★★ Over $20
Dress codes apply in most nightclubs.

BiKiNiS
As the title suggests, the waitresses here wear bikinis, while the waiters serve you in swimming trunks. This all-round indoor beach party also offers water features, jacuzzis and 'exhibition showers' where the staff 'perform'.
Rio All-Suite Hotel & Casino, 3700 W.

Dancers at Tangerine, TI

Flamingo Rd. Tel: (702) 777 6582. Open: 10pm–close. Admission★★/★★★★.

Coyote Ugly Bar & Dance Saloon
Based on the legendary bar in New York, immortalised in the film *Coyote Ugly*, female bartenders dance on the stage and encourage other females to join them. Men have to stay on the floor level, which can be pretty riotous around the bar.
New York–New York Hotel & Casino, 3790 Las Vegas Blvd S. Tel: (702) 740 6969. Open: nightly 6pm–4am. Admission★★/★★★.

Ghostbar
Ghostbar is a very popular nightclub so expect long queues at the weekends, but it is worth the wait. When you reach the 55th floor, with its futuristic interior and three glass walls, the 180° view is breathtaking.
The Palms, 4321 W. Flamingo Road. Tel: (702) 938 2666. Open: nightly 8pm–4am. Admission★★/★★★★.

Late Night at the House of Blues
This live-music venue and nightclub has standing area and a seated balcony. Flashback Fridays offer the best of the

70s, 80s and 90s, then Boogie Nights take you back to the days of disco on Saturday.
Mandalay Bay Resort & Casino, 3950 Las Vegas Blvd S. Tel: (702) 632 7777. Admission★★/★★★. Check current show schedules for your visit.

RA

With two bars, a VIP area and a dance floor surrounded by booths and tables, this is one of the most popular nightclubs in Vegas and welcomes the world's top DJs.
Luxor Hotel & Casino, 3900 Las Vegas Blvd S. Tel: (702) 992 7970. Open: Wed–Sat 10pm–early am. Admission: men★★★ women★★.

Risqué de Paris

This chic after-dinner nightspot offers couches, beds and ottomans surrounding the dance floor and seven private balconies overlooking the strip.
Paris Las Vegas, 3655 Las Vegas Blvd S. Tel: (702) 946 4589. Open: Thur–Sun 10pm–4am. Admission★★★★.

Studio 54

Based on the legendary Studio 54 in New York that dominated the club scene in the 1970s, this Vegas club features retro, progressive and dance music with live dancers and acrobats.
MGM Grand, 3799 Las Vegas Blvd S. Tel: (702) 992 7970. Open: Tue–Sat 10pm–early am. Admission: from★★★★.

Tangerine Lounge and Nightclub

Decorated in warm amber colours and overlooking Sirens cove, this new club features waitresses dressed in lingerie and nightly burlesque performances.
TI, 3300 Las Vegas Blvd S. Tel: (702) 894 7111. Open: Tue–Sat 6pm–4am. Admission: men★★★ women★★.

Coyote Ugly Bar and Dance Saloon

Wedding chapels

Join Brigitte Bardot, Joan Collins, Vic Damon, Bing Crosby, Tony Curtis and countless celebrities who took their wedding vows Las Vegas style. Today the city is known as the wedding capital of the world, where the Clark County Marriage License Bureau states that 'All wedding parties are considered celebrities to us.'

You must obtain a licence to marry in Las Vegas. See pp98–9 for more details.

Vegas' original wedding chapel

HOTEL WEDDING CHAPELS
Bellagio wedding chapels

With a choice of two beautiful chapels, the happy couple can also enjoy the Terrazza di Sogno, a balcony overlooking the lake and fountains.
Bellagio, 3600 Las Vegas Blvd S. Tel: (702) 693 7700. www.bellagio.com

Caesars Palace

With Roman characters and landscaping, themed or traditional weddings are

Viva Las Vegas Wedding Chapel

available in this legendary setting.
Caesars Palace, 3570 Las Vegas Blvd S. Tel: (702) 731 7422.
www.caesarspalace.com

Paris Las Vegas

This beautiful hotel offers the ornate Chapelle du Paradis, the smaller Chapelle du Jardin or a poolside wedding, before the happy couple toast their future at the top of the Eiffel Tower.
Paris Las Vegas, 3655 Las Vegas Blvd S. Tel: (702) 946 7000.
www.parislasvegas.com

Planet Hollywood wedding chapels

With beautiful hand-painted features, the larger of these two new Mediterranean-style chapels can seat up to 60 guests. Elvis and Priscilla Presley were married in the Aladdin Hotel, which was originally on this site, so it's not surprising that the packages include a Love Me Tender option among many others.
Planet Hollywood, 3667 Las Vegas Blvd S. Tel: (866) 945 5933.
www.planethollywood.com

Rio wedding chapels
Choose from the Gardenia, Rio Roses, or Lily of the Valley rooms, then celebrate your wedding with a carnival theme at the Rio.
Rio All-Suite Hotel & Casino, 3700 W. Flamingo Rd. Tel: (702) 777 7986. www.playrio.com

Venetian wedding chapels
Choose from the resort chapel, a gondola ceremony or the Rialto Bridge, where a kiss brings everlasting love.
Venetian Resort Hotel & Casino, 3355 Las Vegas Blvd S. Tel: (702) 414 4280. www.venetianweddings.com

INDEPENDENT WEDDING CHAPELS
Little Chapel of the Flowers
Offering three chapels and beautiful grounds, this popular chapel is located

Over 125,000 couples marry in Las Vegas each year

to the north of the Strip, opposite the Stratosphere.
1717 Las Vegas Blvd S. Tel: (702) 735 4331. www.littlechapel.com

Little Church of the West
Highly recommended, this was the first wedding chapel on the Strip and the beautiful old building stands away from the crowds on the southern tip of Las Vegas Boulevard.
4617 Las Vegas Blvd S. Tel: (702) 739 7971. www.littlechurchlv.com

Maverick Helicopters
Marry over the Las Vegas Strip, on Mount Charleston, at scenic Red Rock Canyon or at the bottom of the Grand Canyon. There are also packages for guests.
Maverick Helicopter Tours, 6075 Las Vegas Blvd S. Tel: (888) 261 0007. www.maverickhelicopter.com

Star Trek Weddings
Marry on board the USS *Enterprise*, with several packages that include the *Captain's Wedding* and *Vulcan Vow Renewal.*
Star Trek: The Experience. The Las Vegas Hilton, 3000 Paradise Rd. Tel: (702) 732 5111. www.startrektheexp.com

Wee Kirk o' the Heather
Opened in 1940, this charming venue was the first Las Vegas wedding chapel; it is also known as the friendliest.
231 Las Vegas Blvd S. Tel: (702) 382 9830. www.weekirk.com

Children in Las Vegas

Over the years, Las Vegas has grown as a family-friendly environment. Free attractions such as the MGM Lion Habitat or the Mirage Volcano will draw crowds of all ages, but the city does not claim to be marketing to children. As visitor numbers have increased, over 10 per cent of tourists are under the age of 21 and too young to indulge in the county's main source of revenue.

Circus Circus Marquee

The city has been described as hospitable to families, but has not made any determined effort to encourage them in its promotional material, although there are many attractions, several suitable resorts and child-care facilities to make your stay in Las Vegas enjoyable for the whole family.

Family-friendly resorts include Circus Circus, with its Adventuredome Theme Park, live circus acts and arcades, and the MGM Grand, with its free Lion Habitat and Youth Activity Center for guests. Further south on the Strip, the Luxor has the IMAX theatre, motion rides and arcades, while the Excalibur features the free *Excalibur Castle Moat Show* and hourly processions with court jesters and entertainers. New York–New York offers the *Manhattan Express* rollercoaster and arcades, while teens will enjoy the *Speedway Motion Rides* at the Sahara.

Resorts not suitable for children include the Bellagio, which does not allow any visitors under the age of 18 to enter its premises, Caesars Palace, the Hard Rock Hotel, Riviera, Stardust or

Dinosaur displays at the Las Vegas Natural History Museum.
See p139

There are strict gaming laws in Las Vegas. Visitors under the age of 21 are prohibited from loitering in or around any area where any licensed gaming is conducted, and cannot play, place bets or collect winnings. The legal age for the consumption or purchase of alcohol is also 21.

the Palms. The Palms does offer day-care facilities, but the hotel attracts many bachelor parties, and promotes an adult theme throughout.

Adults must accompany children under 12 to shopping malls and game arcades, even if they are in a group, and under-16s should not be out alone. On the Strip, there is a 9pm curfew for under-18s, unless accompanied by a parent or guardian.

Day-care facilities in the city include the *Scandia Family Fun Center* for 3–12 year olds, featuring go-carts, bumper boats, mini golf and over 100 games. *Kids Quest!* facilities can be found in the Palms and the Station group of casinos for children aged from 6 weeks–12 years. Activities include its Ballocity Adventure game, spiral slides, ball pits, non-violent video entertainment, arts, crafts and virtual karaoke.

In the Orleans and the South Coast casinos, *Kid's Tyme Centers* offer jungle gyms, arts and crafts, movie rooms and interactive play for children aged 3–9 years. The Hyatt at Lake Las Vegas offers *Camp Hyatt* for ages 3–9 years, with activities that include field games, swimming and water slides, arts, crafts and toad and lizard hunting.

Scandia Family Fun Centre. *2900 Sirius Ave. Tel: (702) 364 0700.*

Kids Quest. *Available at all the Station Casinos or visit www.kidsquest.com*

Kid's Tyme Centers. *The Orleans. 4500 W. Tropicana Ave. Tel: (702) 365 7111; the Southcoast Hotel and Casino: 9777 Las Vegas Blvd S. Tel: (702) 796 7111.*

Camp Hyatt. *Hyatt Regency, 101 Montelago Blvd, Lake Las Vegas. Tel: (702) 567 1234.*

Many resorts can arrange outside babysitting services.

The 10.5-m (35-ft) long Tyrannosaurus Rex even roars at onlookers

Attractions for children

In and around Las Vegas there are many attractions that children will find fascinating, and many of them are free. Most hotels also offer games areas such as Carnival Midway at Circus Circus and the Coney Island Emporium in New York–New York.

See pp134–5, 136–7 & 142–5 for more attractions.

M&M World Marquee

Price guide:
★   Under $5
★★ $5–$10
★★★ Over $10

Adventuredome Theme Park
Fun for all ages, including a rollercoaster, bumper cars, funhouse and virtual-reality zones housed within the largest indoor theme park in the world.
Circus Circus Hotel & Casino, 2880 Las Vegas Blvd S. Tel: (702) 794 3939. Open: Mon–Thur 11am–6pm, Fri & Sat 10am–midnight, Sun 10am–8pm. There

are height restrictions on some of the rides. Ride prices from★. All-day passes available: prices depend on height.

Ethel M Chocolate Factory & Cactus Gardens
Who can ask for anything more than a free tour of a chocolate factory? The botanical gardens also feature over 350 species of desert flora.
2 Cactus Garden Drive, Henderson. Tel: (702) 433 2500. Open: daily 8.30am–7pm. Admission: free.

GameWorks
Including a 23-m (75-ft) rock-climbing pillar, video games, interactive entertainment and refreshments, this is one of the best arcades on the Strip.
3769 Las Vegas Blvd S. Tel: (702) 432 4263. Open: daily 10am–midnight, Fri & Sat until 1am. Admission: free, games priced individually.

Lied Discovery Children's Museum
Education through play. Learn about gravity with

World of Coca-Cola, GameWorks and M&M World on the Strip

Performing dolphins at the Mirage

weight boots, compose music, put mathematics to use and try communication systems among many interactive and educational activities. *833 Las Vegas Blvd N. Tel: (702) 382 3445. Open: Tue–Sun 10am–5pm. Admission: adults★★ children★.*

M&M World

Features M&M merchandise, a 3D movie, the M&M Academy – and offers every colour M&M in production. *Located in the Showcase Mall on the Strip. 3785 Las Vegas Blvd S. Tel: (702) 736 7611. Open: 9am–11pm, Fri & Sat until midnight. Attractions run 10am–6pm, Fri & Sat until 8pm. Admission: free.*

Pharaoh's Pavilion

Attractions include the IMAX 3D Theater, the Tomb and Museum of King Tut and the Games of the Gods Arcade, which features the *Maxflight VR2002*

programmable rollercoaster, video games and interactive machines such as an *Indy 500* racing simulator or the *Xtreme Powerboat.* *Luxor Hotel & Casino, 3900 Las Vegas Blvd S. Tel: (702) 262 4000. Pharaoh's Pavilion open daily 9am–1am, Games of the Gods Arcade open 9am–11pm, Fri & Sat until midnight. Admission: free, with all games and attractions priced individually.*

Ron Lee's World of Clowns

See how Ron Lee creates all his celebrated clown sculptures. Located 20 minutes' drive from the Strip. *330 Carousel Parkway, Henderson. Tel: (702) 434 1700. Mon–Fri 8am–4pm. Admission: free.*

Wizards Arcade

With games of skill for all the family such as darts and milk-bottle pitching, along with virtual-reality machines and interactive games. *Excalibur Hotel & Casino, 3850 Las Vegas Blvd S. Tel: (702) 597 7700. Open: daily 10.30am–11.30pm, Fri & Sat until 1am. Admission: free, games priced individually.*

Siegfried and Roy's beloved animal kingdom

Sport and leisure

There are many sports and recreational facilities in Las Vegas and the surrounding areas, such as Red Rock Canyon, The Grand Canyon and Mount Charleston, which all offer outdoor activities from biking, climbing and watersports to backcountry adventures. Las Vegas is also famed for its championship golf courses and leading sports events from boxing and basketball to rodeo challenges, while race fans will find many events and activities at the Las Vegas Motor Speedway.

Las Vegas Motor Speedway

Escape from the neon and enjoy the breathtaking countryside by taking part in many outdoor activities, for all levels of fitness.

Aerial activities
Take a relaxing balloon tour or visit one of the many parachute and skydiving centres around Las Vegas. Beginners can also try skydiving indoors. *See pp158–61 for more details.*

Fishing
Lake Mead offers hundreds of miles of fishing shores offering bass, catfish, sunfish and rainbow trout among other species. For information on fishing licences contact the Nevada Division of Wildlife: *www.nevadadivisionofwildlife.org. See pp158–61 for more details.*

Hiking
Most ambitious hikers would head straight for the Grand Canyon, but closer to Vegas in the Mount Charleston Wilderness there are several advanced

trails ranging from 13–26km (8–16 miles), reaching elevations of 2,348–3,633m (7,705–11,918ft). All levels including

You'll find good windsurfing conditions at Lake Mead

beginners can visit Red Rock Canyon, which offers 22 trails reaching elevations up to 2,130m (7,000ft), along with the bright red sands of the Valley of Fire State Park, with easier hikes where you can view 3,000-year-old Native American petroglyphs.

Horse riding

Horse riders can visit the fiery Red Rock Canyon, or Mount Charleston and the Spring Mountains National Recreation Area. These trails are very difficult and overnight camping with horses is not allowed.

There are countless routes for keen cyclists

Mountain and road biking

Advanced mountain riders can enjoy the Bootleg Canyon Trails in the Boulder City area, a scenic route that includes the steep 22 per cent Elevator Shaft, the 22-km (14-mile) Elvis Presta Trail network in Spring Mountains and the gruelling 8-km (5-mile) Hurl in Red Rock Canyon. Easier routes include the Old Spanish Trail in Red Rock Canyon and the River Mountains Loop Trail in Henderson. Road cyclists can take it easy on the Red Rock Canyon Scenic Loop or the 80-km (50-mile) Blue Diamond Loop in Spring Mountain Ranch State Park.

Rock climbing

Experienced climbers can enjoy over 1,200 named routes in Red Rock Canyon, along with Mount Charleston, which also offers ice climbing from

2,400m (8,000ft). There are several indoor climbing venues in Las Vegas and centres that offer tuition. *See pp158–61 for more information.*

Skiing and snowboarding

With fresh snow on Mount Charleston and the Spring Mountains it's hard to believe you are in the middle of the desert. Trails are suitable for downhill and cross-country skiers.

Watersports

Lake Mead, the Colorado River and Lake Mohave are all excellent areas for kayaking and canoeing, while the stretch of river between the Hoover Dam and Lake Mohave is perfect for white-water rafting. Scuba divers of all levels can dive in both Lake Mohave and Lake Mead, where divers can also explore a cement tank used for the construction of the Hoover Dam.

Golf courses

Southern Nevada is home to over 60 public or semi-private golf courses with unrivalled views, beautiful landscaping and lush foliage. Over 600,000 rounds of golf are played in the Las Vegas area each year and the city has also hosted major golfing events including the LPGA Seniors Tour, the PGA tour and the NCAA Championships. Tiger Woods achieved his first PGA victory in Las Vegas, which has also welcomed amateur golfers such as former US President Bill Clinton and basketball hero Michael Jordan.

Tee time in Las Vegas

Starting prices per round:
★   Under $50
★★ $50–$100
★★★ $100–$200
★★★★ Over $200
Prices increase at weekends and in peak season.

Angel Park Golf Course★★
Designed by Arnold Palmer and featuring two championship courses, a floodlit driving range and the Cloud Nine lighted par-3 course.
100 South Rampart. Tel: (702) 254 4653. www.angelpark.com

Badlands Golf Club★★
This dramatic course, which takes in the scenic washes and canyons of the desert, was named one of Nevada's Top Ten courses by *Golf Digest* magazine.
9119 Alta Drive. Tel: (702) 363 0754. www.badlandsgc.com

Bali Hai Golf Club★★★★
Designed by Lee Schmidt and Brian Curley, with swaying palm trees over luscious fairways and white granite, Bali Hai's clubhouse is located at the Mandalay Bay site.
5160 Las Vegas Blvd. Tel: (702) 450 8000. www.balihaigolfclub.com

Bear's Best★★★
With views of the Las Vegas skyline and the Red Rock Mountains, Jack Nicklaus designed Bear's Best after designing 100 other courses. Bear's Best features replicas of the 18 best holes created by Nicklaus.
11111 West Flamingo Ave. Tel: (702) 804 8500. www.bearsbest.com

Callaway Golf Center/Giant Golf Academy★
Home to the Divine Nine course with waterfalls and desert vegetation, which is lit by night, this centre also includes a driving range overlooking the Strip and the Danny Gans Junior Golf Academy, which offers free golf tuition for ages 11 to 16.
Corner of Las Vegas Blvd and Sunset Road. Tel: (702) 896 4100.

The Falls Golf Club★★★
This beautiful course at Lake Las Vegas offers waterfalls, water features, panoramic views of the Las Vegas Strip and a Tuscan-themed clubhouse.
101 Via Vin Santo. Tel: (702) 740 5258. www.lakelasvegas.com

Las Vegas Golf Club★★
One of the oldest courses in Las Vegas and host to the Las Vegas City Amateur, the record on this friendly par-72 course is Monte Money's 58.
4300 West Washington. Tel: (702) 646 3003.

Painted Desert★★
Past host of the Nevada Open, this course forsakes green landscaping for natural desert vegetation, with cactus and mesquite, the first of its kind in Las Vegas.

5555 Painted Mirage Way. Tel: (702) 645 2880. www.americangolf.com

Reflection Bay Golf Club
Host to Wendy's Three-Tour Challenge, this 18-hole course was designed by Jack Nicklaus and is located at Lake Las Vegas. Some of the holes play along the shoreline.
72 Montelago Blvd, Henderson. Tel: (702) 740 4653. Call for prices. www.lakelasvegas.com

The Wynn Golf and Country Club
This new world-class golf course was designed by Tom Fazio and features a par-70 course where 11 out of 18 holes have water features.
Wynn Las Vegas, 3131 Las Vegas Blvd S. Tel: (702) 770 7000. Call for prices.

Angel Park Golf Course

Desert activities

Enjoy the great outdoors, with extreme sports, recreational activities, tours and cruises in the desert area surrounding Las Vegas. Some of these companies may arrange transfers from Las Vegas. Check your hotel box office, or local magazines, for details on more tours and excursions.

Jet-ski on Lake Mead

Adventure Balloons
Offering early-morning hot-air balloon rides from the Las Vegas Strip to the mountains, their flagship balloon *Smile High* can carry up to eight passengers. *PO Box 27466, Las Vegas 89126. Tel: (702) 247 6905. www.smilerides.com*

Adventure Photo Tours
Tours include photo safari tours in the Mohave Desert, where you can see Aztec sandstone formations, ancient Indian petroglyphs and pictographs, arches, gold mines, ghost towns, wild animals and desert flora. *3111 South Valley View Blvd, X-106. Tel: (702) 889 8687.*

All American Adventure Tours
Tours include the Grand Canyon, Hoover Dam, Indian Country, Colorado rafting, Lake Mead cruises, off-road tours and horse riding. *Transfers from Las Vegas. Tel: (702) 876 4600. www.americanadventuretours.com*

Angler's Edge Guide Service
Offering guided fishing trips on Lake Mohave and Lake Mead, stocked with a wide variety of game fish. *915 Horse Trails Ave, Henderson. Tel: (702) 285 2814. www.fishanglersedge.com*

Cowboy Trail Rides
Offering horse rides such as the Sunset Ride and BBQ in Red Rock Canyon, where you can enjoy steaks cooked on the campfire as you overlook the city of Las Vegas.

Pretend you're a cowboy on a trail ride

Located close to Downtown Las Vegas
with transfers from the Strip. Tel: (702)
387 2457. www.cowboytrailrides.com

Eagle Rider Motorcycle Rental
Rent a shiny new Harley-Davidson and
cruise across Nevada on models such as
the Road King, Electra Glide, or the Fat
Boy with its shotgun-style dual exhaust.
5182 South Arville St (2 blocks south of
the Orleans Hotel & Casino). Tel: (702)
876 8687. www.egleriderlasvegas.com

Extraterrestrial Highway
Passing close to Area 51, the world's
most secret air base where ET hunters
claim that UFOs are tested and flown.
Stop for a snack at the world-famous
Little A'Le'Inn, but keep your eyes
skyward!
Nevada Route 375, Rachel, NV. The ET
Highway is noticeably marked.

www.littlealeinn.com
Most tour operators offer Area 51 packages.

First Travel Tours
Offering tours to the Grand Canyon,
Bryce Canyon and the mysterious Area
51. Adventure tours include white-water
rafting on the Colorado and sunset
horseback dinner rides.
3001 Lake East Drive #1021. Tel: (702)
228 9902. www.firsttraveltours.com

Fish Vegas
Chartered fishing trips on Lake Mead
with master guide Captain Mike.
1547 Irene Drive, Boulder City.
Tel: (702) 293 6294.
www.fishvegas.com

Forever Resorts
Offering boat charters, resorts and
lodging, fishing and rafting cruises and

Rent a Harley and glide through the desert

conference facilities around the Colorado River, Lake Mead and throughout the US.
www.foreverresorts.com

Grand Canyon Tour Company

Try their spooky Ghost Town and Gold Mine tour, or a selection of air, bus, helicopter, hiking or train tours that include the Grand Canyon, Lake Mead and the Hoover Dam.
Tel: (702) 655 6060.
www.grandcanyontourcompany.com

Lake Mead Cruises

Voted by *Nevada Magazine* readers as 'Best Adventure Tour Company in Nevada'. Cruises aboard their Mississippi-style paddle wheelers include a midday sightseeing cruise, an early dinner cruise and a dinner dance cruise. They also cater for weddings.

The scenic Colorado River

PO Box 62465, Boulder City. Tel: (702) 293 6180. www.lakemeadcruises.com

Las Vegas Boat Harbor Inc

This family business has operated on Lake Mead since 1957 and offers all-year-round boating, a café and a marine and tackle store. Powerboats, pontoon boats and jet-skis are all available for rental. This is the closest marina to Las Vegas.
490 Horsepower Cove, Boulder City.
Tel: (702) 293 1191.
www.boatinglakemead.com

Las Vegas Mini Grand Prix

Ten adults (aged 16+) can race around the longest go-kart track in Nevada, while their positions are displayed on an electronic timing board. A Kiddie Kart track is also available for children.
1401 North Rainbow Blvd.
Tel: (702) 259 7000.
www.lvmgp.com.
Open: daily 10am–10pm, Fri & Sat until 11pm.

Las Vegas Motor Speedway

Hosting many high-profile race events, the $200-million Las Vegas Motor Speedway holds 117,000 grandstand seats. The complex features a 2.4-km (1^1/$_2$-mile) super speedway Tri Oval with a 4-km (2^1/$_2$-mile) road course, along with a dirt oval, a paved oval,

a dragway, a paved Legends Cars track, go-kart and off-road facilities.
7000 Las Vegas Blvd N. Tel: (702) 644 4443. www.lvms.com

Maverick Helicopter Tours
With an exclusive landing area in the Grand Canyon, Maverick offer several tours of the canyon and night flights over Las Vegas.
6075 Las Vegas Blvd S. Tel: (702) 261 0007. www.maverickhelicopter.com

Neptune Divers of Southern Nevada
Dive sites include the 13.7-m (45-ft) cruiser *Toruga* in the Boulder Islands dive park, the Cement Factory for more experienced divers, and the Scuba Park, which has seven underwater sites including a sailing boat, cement tube and truck cab.
5831 East Lake Mead Blvd. Tel: (702) 452 5723. www.nevada-scuba.com

Powerhouse Rock Climbing Center
This indoor climbing centre offers 836sq m (9,000sq ft) of climbing space and caters for beginners and advanced climbers, offering group lessons or personal tuition.
8201 W Charleston Blvd #B. Tel: (702) 254 5604. Open: Mon–Fri 11am–10pm, Sat & Sun 9am–9pm.

Richard Petty Driving Experience
Not within every visitor's budget, this is strictly for race-car fans. Ride along in a stock car, driven by a professional instructor, try eight laps on your own in a Winston Cup car, or choose 16- to 80-lap advanced programmes, all with tuition.

6975 Speedway Blvd, Unit D-106. Tel: (800) BE-PETTY. Open: Mon–Fri 8.30am–7.30pm, Sat & Sun 10am–4pm (EST). The booking office is on the east coast of the United States.

Rocky Trails
Adventurous tours that include ATV quad four-wheeler tours, horse riding, kayaking below Hoover Dam, rafting, hiking in Red Rock Canyon and mountain biking.
1930 Village Center Circle 3-155. Tel: (702) 869 9991. www.rockytrails.com

Sky's The Limit
The largest indoor climbing centre in Nevada, offering 1,300sq m (14,000sq ft) of climbing walls for all levels. They also provide a guide service for those wishing to explore the outdoor ranges in the area.
HCR Box 1, Calico Basin. Tel: (702) 363 4533.

FURTHER INFORMATION

Grand Canyon National Park.
www.nps.gov/graca/grandcanyon

Red Rock Canyon National Conservation Area. *Tel: (702) 363 1921. www.redrockcanyon.blm.gov*

Spring Mountains National Recreation Area. *Tel: (702) 873 8800. www.fs.fed.us/htnf*

Valley of Fire State Park. *Tel: (702) 397 2088. www.state.nv.us/stparks*

See pp114–17 for more details of these areas.

Health clubs and spas

It is not all about late nights and all-you-can-eat buffets. You can also look after yourself in Las Vegas with an indulgent visit to a health spa. Daily visits range from $15 to $50 but there may be discounts available for resort guests, and spa packages are often available when you arrange your hotel booking.

Take time to chill out

Canyon Ranch Spa Club

Locals and visitors to Las Vegas claim this is the best day spa in the city. Its countless features include weight-training and cycling gyms, classes, personal training, leading-edge cardio and a 12-m (40-ft) rock-climbing wall.
Venetian Resort Hotel and Casino, 3355 Las Vegas Blvd S. Tel: (702) 414 3600. Open: daily 5.30am–10pm.

Elemis Spa at Aladdin

With steam rooms, saunas, whirlpools, fitness equipment and trainers, the Elemis also offers a beauty salon and treatments that include the Hawaiian wave massage, Thai massage, Balinese massage, Indian Ayurvedic, reflexology, shiatsu and reiki.
Aladdin Resort & Casino, 3667 Las Vegas Blvd S. Tel: (702) 785 5555. Open: daily 6am–7pm.

The MGM Grand Spa

Enjoy Vegas-style body massages such as the margarita salt scrub, cosmopolitan cranberry or pina colada. There is a full-service salon and amenities include whirlpools, sauna, steam rooms, a fitness centre and pool.
MGM Grand, 3799 Las Vegas Blvd S. Tel: (702) 891 3077. Open: daily 6am–8pm.

The Oasis Spa at Luxor

Enjoy body wraps, facials and treatments including pumpkin enzyme peel, cranberry enzyme scrub, hazelnut body masque, sports and reflexology massage 24 hours a day. Full body tanning is also available.
Luxor Hotel & Casino, 3900 Las Vegas Blvd S. Tel: (702) 730 4444. Open: 6am–8pm.

The Rock Spa

Feel like a pampered rock star with the fabulous spa and salon packages available at the Hard Rock. Make full use of the steam rooms, jacuzzi and fitness room and enjoy treatments that include deep tissue massage, reflexology and facials.
Hard Rock Hotel & Casino, 4455 Paradise Road. Tel: (702) 693 5554. Open: daily 6am–10pm.

The Spa at Caesars Palace

Treatments include Moor mud baths, sea salt treatments and body wraps. You can relax by the pool or enjoy the juice bar,

saunas, whirlpool and lounges. The fitness centre also includes a climbing wall.
Caesars Palace, 3570 Las Vegas Blvd S. Tel: (702) 731 7776. Open: daily 6am–8pm. Outside guests only Fri & Sat.

Spa Mandalay

This beautiful oasis offers a full-service salon and treatments that include the Epicurean facial, cocoa butter wrap, papaya mango scrub, outdoor massages and even yoga on the beach.
Mandalay Bay Resort & Casino, 3950 Las Vegas Blvd S. Tel: (702) 632 7220. Open: daily 6am–8.30pm.

Spa by Mandara

This busy spa offers deep tissue, Swedish, aromatique and couples massages as well as treatments for pregnant women. There is also a full-service salon.
Paris Las Vegas, 3655 Las Vegas Blvd S. Tel: (702) 946 4366. Open: daily 7am–7pm, Fri & Sat 5am–9pm.

The Spa at Monte Carlo

This elegant spa offers massages, body scrubs, wraps, waxing, facials and detox treatments. Amenities include whirlpools, sauna, steam rooms, relaxation room, fitness centre and full-service saloon.
Monte Carlo, 3770 Las Vegas Blvd S. Tel: (702) 730 7590. Open: daily 6am–9pm.

The Spa at Caesars Palace offers Ayurvedic and Indonesian massages

Along with the luxurious hotel resorts and entertainment, dining is unsurpassed in Las Vegas. When you arrive at McCarran Airport, mouth-watering advertisements boast world-famous chefs and all-you-can-eat buffets in a city that offers 24-hour dining, themed restaurants and gourmet cuisine from every corner of the globe.

All you can eat

Eighty per cent of Las Vegas visitors will opt for the all-you-can-eat-buffet. Offered in almost every resort, diners can choose from seafood, carved meats and international cuisine. The first Las Vegas Buffet was the Midnight Chuck Wagon in the El Rancho during the 1940s.

Themed restaurants

All the main themed eating establishments have some of their flagship restaurants in Las Vegas. Look out for the original Planet Hollywood in Caesars Palace, the Hard Rock Café, the Harley-Davidson Café and the Rainforest Café. Star Trek fans can dine in Quark's Bar and Restaurant at the Las Vegas Hilton, while motorsports fanatics can enjoy the NASCAR Café at the Sahara.

Seafood

Enjoy the culinary creations of chef Emeril Lagasse at the New Orleans Fish House at the MGM Grand and Tom Maloney's AquaKnox at the Venetian. Seafood is on many buffet menus, particularly at the Paradise Garden Buffet at the Flamingo and the Market Square Buffet at Harrah's. Las Vegas also offers countless oyster bars, lobster houses and sushi bars such as the Hyakumi Japanese Restaurant & Sushi Bar at Caesars Palace or Sushi King at the Stardust.

All American

Las Vegas is famed for its steak houses and prime-rib specials.

Enjoy the glamour and atmosphere of old Las Vegas in AJ's Steakhouse at the Hard Rock Hotel, or try the celebrated Charlie Palmer Steak House at the Four Seasons. The Loft at the Orleans offers excellent prime rib, while you can get a 450-g (16-oz) steak 24 hours a day at the Gold Coast's Monterey Room.

Fine dining

While Picasso and Le Cirque at Bellagio and Renoir at the Mirage have all earned Mobil five-star ratings, Las Vegas offers countless gourmet restaurants to satisfy the most discerning palate. Top chefs including André Rochat, Jean-Marie Josselin and Sirio Maccioni are among the many world-famous chefs who offer their gourmet delights in Las Vegas, along with the celebrated Wolfgang Puck with establishments such as Chinois, Postrio Trattoria del Lupo and his Hollywood institution Spago.

Loosen that belt...

Your choice is endless. You can eat breakfast 24 hours a day, or choose from a world of cuisines that include American, Asian, Brazilian, Chinese, Cuban, French, Indian, Indonesian, Irish, Italian, Japanese, Mexican, Moroccan, Persian and Vietnamese. And to wash it all down, Las Vegas is home to 12 of the 56 US master sommeliers and establishments which have earned critical acclaim for their wine lists.

Opposite: A world of possibilities at the Fashion Show Mall
Above: Andre's French restaurant in the Monte Carlo

The Las Vegas buffet

With dishes from around the world, Las Vegas is famed for its all-you-can-eat buffets. Be prepared to put on a little weight after returning to fill your plate time after time, as there is so much to choose from and most restaurants offer breakfast, lunch and evening selections.

All you can eat!

Price guide per person, for dinner (excluding tax and gratuities):
★   Under $15
★★ $15–$20
★★★   Over $20

Most hotels offer a buffet and serve breakfast from 7am, lunch from 11.30am and dinner from the late afternoon, usually between 4pm and 5pm.

The Buffet at the Golden Nugget★★
Known for its Sunday champagne brunch and its carved meats, the Golden Nugget is a popular buffet located in the centre of Downtown Las Vegas.
Golden Nugget Hotel, 129 East Fremont Street. Tel: (702) 385 7111.

The Buffet – Las Vegas Hilton★★
Just off the Strip, this buffet offers fresh fruit, salads and delicious main courses including a carving station, followed by desserts prepared by world-renowned pastry chef Stanton Ho. Champagne brunches are also available.
Las Vegas Hilton, 3000 Paradise Road. Tel: (702) 732 5111.

Carnival World Buffet★★★
Voted the best buffet in Las Vegas, with more than 300 freshly prepared dishes including Italian, Asian, barbecue and sushi, with live cooking stations and over 70 varieties of homemade pies, cakes and pastries.
Rio All-Suite Hotel & Casino, 3700 W. Flamingo Road. Tel: (702) 777 7777.

Circus Circus Buffet★
One of the largest in Las Vegas, this buffet is also one of the most reasonable and breakfast here is very popular.
Circus Circus, 2880 Las Vegas Blvd S. Tel: (702) 734 0410.

Cravings★★★
Wander through streets lined with restaurants within a beautiful village setting, with eleven cooking stations and live cooking broadcasts and cuisine from across the world.
The Mirage, 3400 Las Vegas Blvd S. Tel: (702) 791 7111.

Feast Around the World Buffet★★
Dinner includes prime rib and seafood and many food stations offering a huge variety of dishes. This resort is featured on the television reality show American Casino. Highly recommended.
Green Valley Ranch Resort and Spa. 2300 Paseo Verde Pkwy, Henderson. Tel: (702) 617 7777.

Le Village Buffet – Paris Las Vegas★★★

This highly acclaimed buffet includes sweet and savoury crêpes, delicious main courses, seafood, cheeses and freshly baked French breads all in a beautiful village setting.
Paris Las Vegas, 3655 Las Vegas Blvd S. Tel: (877) 796 2096.

MGM Grand Buffet★★

All you can eat Hollywood-style with carving stations, seafood, a bountiful salad bar and mouth-watering desserts. The MGM Grand also offers a weekend champagne brunch.
MGM Grand Hotel & Casino, 3799 Las Vegas Blvd S. Tel: (702) 891 1111.

Paradise Garden Buffet★★

Known for its seafood, steaks and salmon dishes, this buffet looks out on the Flamingo lagoon areas.
Flamingo Las Vegas, 3555 Las Vegas Blvd S. Tel: (702) 733 3111.

The Pharaoh's Pheast Buffet★★

This popular buffet offers a 9-m (30-ft) salad bar, homemade pizza station, two carving stations, two omelette stations and dishes from around the world.
Luxor Hotel & Casino, 3900 Las Vegas Blvd S. Tel: (702) 262 4000.

There are dishes from around the world at Cravings

Food and drink

A 24-hour city attracting millions of visitors from all corners of the globe needs to offer an extensive selection of restaurants and cuisine. Whether you want fine dining, American home cooking, Japanese, Mexican, Moroccan or Italian, there are hundreds of establishments to choose from in Las Vegas. Pick up a local *What's On* guide or similar publication as soon as you arrive to find offers and information on the city's best eating spots.

Monte Carlo Pub & Brewery

Price guide per person, for a main course:

★   Under $10
★★ $10–$20
★★★ $21–$30
★★★★ Over $30

Joe's in the Forum Shops at Caesars Palace

Café Ba-Ba-Reeba★★

Choose from a wide variety of authentic Spanish tapas and share paella, calderos or the cowboy rib eye steak. Follow with mini dessert tapas or the sorbet and liquor *Spanish bull's eyes*.
The Fashion Show Mall, 3200 Las Vegas Blvd S. Tel: (702) 258 1211.
Open: Sun–Thur 11.30am–midnight, Fri & Sat until 2am.

The Cortez Room★★

Just one meal here tells you why the Cortez Room is so popular with locals. Serving American and seafood, the prime rib is excellent, servings are generous and the staff are very friendly.
The Gold Coast Hotel & Casino, 4000 West Flamingo Road. Tel: (702) 367 7111.
Open: Sun–Thur 4–10pm, Fri & Sat until 10.30pm.

Eiffel Tower Restaurant★★★★

Enjoy cocktails or caviar and wonderful French cuisine created by award-winning chef J Joho. Enjoy a great view from this dining room of the Strip 11 storeys up on the Eiffel Tower.
Paris Las Vegas, 3645 Las Vegas Blvd S.

Tel: (702) 948 6937. Open: daily lunch 11am–3pm; dinner Sun–Thur 5–10.15pm, Fri & Sat until 10.45pm.

Fat Burger★★
Located just north of the MGM Grand on the Strip, this popular restaurant serves all-American burger meals in huge portions.
3763 Las Vegas Blvd S. Tel: (702) 736 4733. Open: daily 24 hours.

Gandhi India's Cuisine★★
Voted best Indian meal in Las Vegas and offering tandoori dishes, seafood, meat curries and vegetarian meals, this restaurant also offers an all-you-can-eat lunch buffet.
4080 Paradise Road. Tel: (702) 734 0094. Open: daily, lunch 11am–2pm, dinner 5–10pm.

Garduños at the Palms★★
Mexican cuisine with fajitas, seafood, burritos and an extensive margarita

Fine dining awaits you in Vegas

selection. Garduños also features the Blue Agave Oyster & Chile Bar and offers a Sunday all-you-can-eat margarita brunch.
Palms Casino Resort, 4321 West Flamingo Road. Tel: (702) 942 7777. Open: Mon–Thur 11am–10pm, Fri 11am–10.30pm, Sat noon–10.30pm; Sun 10.30am–10pm, brunch served until 3pm.

Harley-Davidson Café★★
Featuring the largest display of Harley-Davidson memorabilia and American dishes that include pasta, chicken, barbecue, salads and sandwiches. There is also a Harley-Davidson shop in the restaurant.
3725 Las Vegas Blvd S. Tel: (702) 740 4555. Open: Sun–Thur 11am–10pm, Fri & Sat 11am–11pm.

Hyakumi Japanese Restaurant & Sushi Bar★★★★
Translated as '100 tastes', Hyakumi offers 40 varieties of sushi and sashimi along with many other Japanese dishes from the menu. Sit at the sushi bar or have your food prepared at a tableside grill. Highly recommended.
Caesars Palace, 3570 Las Vegas Blvd S. Tel: (702) 731 7731. Open: daily, lunch 11am–3.30pm, dinner 5–11pm.

Landry's Seafood House★★
Landry's have restaurants all over the United States, resembling 1940s seafood houses, and offer huge servings of world-famous seafood specialities, as well as a selection of non-seafare. Excellent value.
2610 West Sahara Ave. Tel: (702) 251 0101. Open: Sun–Thur 10am–10.15pm, Fri & Sat until 11.15pm.

The Lobster House★★★

Located on the Strip across from Monte Carlo, the Lobster House offers fresh seafood from the east and west coasts including live Maine lobster, Alaskan king crab legs and Gulf scampi. *3763 Las Vegas Blvd S. Tel: (702) 740 4431. Open: daily 5–11.30pm.*

Mon Ami Gabi★★

Watch the world rush by on the Strip, or enjoy the *Fountains at Bellagio* while you dine alfresco outside Paris. Wonderful wines complement French cuisine that includes cassoulet, shallot steak and bouillabaisse created by award-winning chef Gabino Sotelino.

Japanese cuisine at Shibuya, MGM Grand

Paris Las Vegas. 3645 Las Vegas Blvd S. Tel: (702) 944 4224. Open: daily, lunch 11.30am–3.30pm, dinner 4–11pm, Fri & Sat until midnight.

Monte Carlo Brew Pub★★
Not listed as a restaurant, but a microbrewery which offers home-made beers, live music and an extensive food menu including pizzas, gourmet wraps and sandwiches.
Monte Carlo Resort & Casino, 3770 Las Vegas Blvd S. Tel: (702) 730 7777. Open: Sun–Fri 11am–3am, Sat 11am–4am. Food is served until 10pm.

N9NE★★★★
Winner of the *Best in Vegas* for 2005, this highly acclaimed steakhouse also features a champagne and caviar bar within an elegant setting, with leather, suede and bright metallic furnishings.
Palms Casino Resort, 4321 W. Flamingo Ave. Tel: (702) 942 7777. Open: Sun–Thur 5–11pm. Fri & Sat until 11.30pm.

Nine Fine Irishmen★★
A popular bar with a hearty menu that is hard to resist. Choose from main courses such as beer-battered fish and chips or shepherd's pie infused with port, then follow up with Bushmills bread pudding with whiskey cream.
New York–New York Hotel and Casino, 3790 Las Vegas Blvd S. Tel: (702) 740 6969. Open: daily, lunch 11am–4pm, dinner 4–11pm.

Rainforest Café★★
With animated elephants and gorillas, waterfalls and a saltwater aquarium, this lively restaurant is popular with all the family and offers American cuisine and the chain's signature dishes.
MGM Grand Hotel & Casino, 3799 Las Vegas Blvd S. Tel: (702) 891 8580. Open: daily 8am–11pm, Fri & Sat until midnight.

Stephanos★★
A beautiful setting in the Downtown Golden Nugget, where the waiters sing to you as you select from Italian dishes such as linguine with clams, scampi fra diavolo and their famed cioppino fisherman's stew. The wine list includes over 200 choices.
The Golden Nugget Hotel, 129 Fremont St. Tel: (702) 385 7111. Open: daily 5.30–11pm.

Tony Roma's★★
Described as the best rib joint in Las Vegas, Tony Roma's also offers flame-grilled steaks, seafood and world-famous onion rings.
Stardust Resort & Casino, 3000 Las Vegas Blvd S. Tel: (702) 732 6500. Open: daily 5–11pm.

Top of the World★★★★
Dress up for the evening and enjoy a meal in one of Las Vegas's top gourmet restaurants. This impressive restaurant offers 360° views of the city from the top of the Stratosphere Tower as it slowly rotates over a period of one hour.
The Stratosphere Tower Hotel & Casino, 2000 Las Vegas Blvd S. Tel: (702) 380 7711. Open: 11am–2.30pm, 5.30–10.15pm, Fri & Sat until 10.45pm.

Hotels and accommodation

In general, room rates in Las Vegas are extremely reasonable, and you pay one price for the room rather than for each person. For the best prices contact the hotels directly, through their booking line, or visit their websites. Rates are higher at the weekend so, for the best prices, incorporate as many weekdays as you can. Standard rooms usually include one king-size bed or two queen beds, which you can choose when booking.

Circus Circus marquee

Price guide, per room:
★   Under $50
★★ $50–$100
★★★ $101–$200
★★★★   Over $200
These prices are based on low season midweek prices for a standard room.

STRIP HOTELS AND RESORTS
Compared to other cities, Las Vegas Strip resorts offer some of the most luxurious hotel rooms for extremely competitive prices.

Bally's Las Vegas★★
This elegant resort with moving walkways to its entrance is in the centre of the Strip. Guest towers include Parlor suites and standard rooms.
3645 Las Vegas Blvd S.
Tel: (702) 739 4111.
www.ballyslv.com

Bellagio★★★★
This AAA Five Diamond award-winning resort overlooks the fountains of Bellagio in the centre of the Strip and features nearly 4,000 opulent guest rooms and suites.
3600 Las Vegas Blvd S.
Tel: (702) 693 7111.
www.bellagio.com

Caesars Palace★★★
A luxurious resort located in the centre of the Strip with some of the finest European-style hotel rooms in Las Vegas.
3570 Las Vegas Blvd S.
Tel: (702) 731 7110.
www.caesarspalace.com

Circus Circus Hotel & Casino★
One of the most family-friendly resorts on the Strip, with over 3,700 rooms; the carnival theme continues in the rooms and suites.
2880 Las Vegas Blvd S.
Tel: (702) 734 0410.
www.circuscircus.com

Excalibur Hotel & Casino★★
Resembling a medieval castle, the Excalibur resort at the south end of the

Strip is another family favourite with a large pool complex.
3850 Las Vegas Blvd S.
Tel: (702) 597 7777.
www.excalibur.com

Flamingo Las Vegas★★
A favourite for regular visitors, with 3,500 rooms, this resort features beautiful lagoons and swimming areas.
3555 Las Vegas Blvd S.
Tel: (702) 733 3111.
www.flamingolasvegas.com

Imperial Palace Hotel & Casino★★
Located in the centre of the Strip and themed on the Orient, rooms include Standard, Penthouse and King suites.
3535 Las Vegas Blvd S.
Tel: (702) 731 3311.
www.imperialpalace.com

Luxor Hotel & Casino★★
This popular family resort towards the south of the Strip features 4,400 rooms, all designed with an Egyptian theme.
2830 Las Vegas Blvd S.
Tel: (702) 262 4000.
www.luxor.com

Suite Calais at Paris offers his and hers baths, a whirlpool and a stunning view of the Strip

Opened in 1993, Luxor now has 4,400 rooms

Mandalay Bay Resort & Casino★★
This South Seas paradise features a luxurious swimming area and bay for its guests, who can choose from more than 3,300 spacious rooms and suites.
3950 Las Vegas Blvd S.
Tel: (702) 632 7777.
www.mandalaybay.com

MGM Grand Hotel & Casino★★★
This is one of the largest hotels in the world and is located on the south end of the Strip with over 5,000 guest rooms.
3799 Las Vegas Blvd S.
Tel: (702) 891 7777.
www.mgmgrand.com

Mirage★★★
This tropical paradise with its own fiery volcano offers nearly 3,000 de luxe rooms and suites and is located right in the centre of the Strip.
3400 Las Vegas Blvd S.
Tel: (702) 791 7111.
www.mirage.com

Monte Carlo★★
Always maintaining a European elegance, the Monte Carlo offers over 3,000 de luxe rooms and suites.
3770 Las Vegas Blvd S.
Tel: (702) 730 7777.
www.montecarlo.com

New York–New York Hotel & Casino★★
The 2,000 guest rooms in this stunning resort are located in skyscraper towers that recreate the Manhattan skyline.
3790 Las Vegas Blvd S.
Tel: (702) 740 6969.
www.nynyhotelcasino.com

Paris Las Vegas★★★
This romantic resort features 3,000 beautiful hotel rooms with luxurious custom-designed furnishings and is located right in the centre of the Strip.
3655 Las Vegas Blvd S.
Tel: (800) 946 7000.
www.parislasvegas.com

Planet Hollywood Hotel and Casino
Formerly the Aladdin Hotel and Casino, this glamorous new hotel is due to be completely renovated by late 2006. It includes 4,000 rooms and apartments, centrally located on the Las Vegas Strip.
3667 Las Vegas Blvd S.
Rates and telephone details to be announced.
www.planethollywood.com

Riviera Hotel & Casino★
It is not as glamorous as its later successors but is conveniently located towards the northern end of the Strip and features 2,100 de luxe guest rooms.
2901 Las Vegas Blvd S.
Tel: (702) 734 5110.
www.theriviera.com

Sahara Hotel & Casino★
Featuring 1,720 recently refurbished guest rooms with a Moroccan motif, the Sahara is at the north end of the Strip.
2535 Las Vegas Blvd S.
Tel: (702) 737 2111.
www.saharavegas.com

Stardust Resort & Casino★★
The Stardust offers 1,500 rooms and suites, with many rooms in the West Tower featuring views of the Vegas skyline.
3000 Las Vegas Blvd S. Tel: (702) 732 6111. www.stardustlv.com

Stratosphere Tower Hotel & Casino★★
With its high-rise space needle the Stratosphere offers 2,444 guest rooms and suites at the northern tip of the Strip.
2000 Las Vegas Blvd S.
Tel: (702) 380 7777.
www.stratospherehotel.com

TI – Treasure Island★★
Appealing more to an adult clientele, rather than the family destination that was first developed, this exciting resort offers 2,885 guest rooms with floor-to-ceiling windows right in the centre of the Strip.
3300 Las Vegas Blvd S.
Tel: (702) 894 7111.
www.treasureisland.com

The Venetian Resort Hotel & Casino★★★
With over 4,000 suites, the rooms at the Venetian are twice the size of standard Vegas rooms, with features such as sunken lounges and canopy-draped king-size beds.
3355 Las Vegas Blvd S.
Tel: (702) 414 1000.
www.venetian.com

OFF-STRIP HOTELS
Resort prices can be a lot cheaper off the Strip, but offer the same standard of accommodation and service. There are also many popular motel chains in the city such as Budget Suites, Hampton Inn and Holiday Inn.

Gold Coast Hotel & Casino★
Southern western-style furnishings and some of the best food just 1.6km (1 mile) west of the Strip. The Gold Coast has 711 rooms and a bowling alley.
4000 West Flamingo Road.
Tel: (702) 367 7111.
www.goldcoastcasino.com

Golden Nugget★★
In the heart of Fremont Street, this ornate hotel features nearly 2,000 guest rooms and was refurbished by developer

Steve Wynn (famed for the Bellagio and Wynn).
129 E Fremont St.
Tel: (702) 385 7111.
www.goldennugget.com

Hard Rock Hotel & Casino★★★

This rock 'n' roll paradise is located only one road east of the Strip. It offers 670 guest rooms and luxury suites and certainly invites a fun-loving crowd.

4455 Paradise Road.
Tel: (702) 693 5000.
www.hardrockhotel.com

Las Vegas Hilton★

Highly recommended, this friendly luxurious resort was once the largest hotel in the world. With 3,000 rooms, the service is excellent.
3000 Paradise Road.
Tel: (702) 732 5111.
www.lvhilton.com

Mandalay Bay, Excalibur and Luxor are all linked by monorail

Ipanema Beach at Rio

The Orleans Hotel & Casino★

A Mardi Gras themed hotel, with over 1,800 rooms, the Orleans is just off the south end of the Strip and also offers a 70-lane bowling alley.

4500 Tropicana Ave.
Tel: (702) 365 7111.
www.orleanscasino.com

Palms Casino Resort★★

This adult themed resort with 455 guest rooms includes dance poles and dance floors in its Playpen suites.

4321 West Flamingo Road.
Tel: (702) 942 7777.
www.palms.com

Rio All-Suite Casino Resort★★★

With 2,500 suites, all with refrigerators and floor-to-ceiling windows offering fantastic views, this Brazilian themed resort is highly recommended and close to the Strip.

3700 West Flamingo Road.
Tel: (702) 252 7777.
www.playrio.com

An ever-evolving city

Where did they go? The Dunes, the Sands, the Desert Inn? Monarchs of the Las Vegas Strip now lost in the clutches of developers. The original Strip hotels are disappearing from Las Vegas at a dramatic rate, as the city constantly rewrites its future in tourism.

The first hotel on the Strip, El Rancho, was lost in a fire in 1960, while the Dunes was 'imploded' (demolished) in October 1993, the Landmark in November 1995 and, after 50 years on the Strip, the Desert Inn finally closed its doors in August 2000. On 25 December 1995, lights throughout Las Vegas were dimmed to mark the death of Dean Martin, but even the historic Sands hotel, famous for its Rat Pack summit, could not fight the development of the city and was imploded in November 1996. The Venetian now stands on the site.

A hotel implosion is an attraction quite unique to Las Vegas. Hotel rooms are filled across the city as people check in to witness the event. Then, on the date of destruction, nearby streets are cleared and a dazzling display of fireworks and dynamite marks the demise of another Las Vegas landmark.

However, the city's ability to evolve has created a progressive and unrivalled tourist destination. As new hotels are

built, older hotels are constantly being refurbished to maintain the luxurious Las Vegas standards. The 40-year-old Hacienda was replaced by the exotic Mandalay Bay, the old Desert Rose Motel made way for the Monte Carlo and the Bellagio replaced the Dunes in 1996. Every new resort seems more impressive, more alluring and more expensive than its predecessors, creating an ever-changing panorama for the repeat visitor.

A recent addition to the Las Vegas strip is Steve Wynn's eagerly awaited Wynn Las Vegas, a multi-billion-dollar mega-resort on the site of the former Desert Inn. In the wake of September 11, the 50-year-old Desert Inn was not imploded, but removed from the strip without ceremony. But Wynn's grand opening in the spring of 2005 was a celebratory affair, as the city of Las Vegas celebrated its first centenary, a brief 100 years since the first plots of land were sold in auction.

One of the city's most beneficial changes was the addition of the *Fremont Street Experience* in 1995. Downtown Las Vegas was often overlooked in favour of the Strip attractions and this multi-million-dollar facelift rejuvenated the area, which was almost in danger of becoming a ghost town.

Compared to other metropolitan areas, Las Vegas is an infant city. It is still growing, still evolving – and most welcoming to any visitors who are keen to chart its progress.

Opposite: Wynn under construction on the former site of the Desert Inn
Above: The Mirage

Practical guide

Entry requirements

Citizens of Australia, New Zealand, Ireland and the UK (as well as citizens of most western European countries and Japan) need only a valid machine-readable passport to enter the USA if their stay is less than 90 days, they have a return ticket and have arrived on an airline participating in the visa-waiver programme (most major carriers). Make sure that your visa-waiver form includes the full address of your first night's accommodation. Canadian citizens need only identification and proof of residence. Citizens of South Africa and most other countries must present a passport and tourist visa. There is now an extra check when you arrive at a US airport – a photograph plus fingerprinting.

Travellers who require visas should obtain them from a US consulate or embassy in their country of residence, as they are difficult to obtain elsewhere. In the UK your Thomas Cook travel consultant can advise.

Route 66 sign

Unless you are flying directly to Las Vegas, it's likely that you will fly into a gateway city first. This first stop will be where you clear immigration and customs. Ensure that your visa-waiver form and customs declaration are completed correctly when you leave the plane, as immigration officials are known for their lack of patience. Details can be found in most airline magazines and flight attendants will also be able to advise you. Once you have cleared immigration, you pick up your luggage and proceed to US Customs. If you have a connecting flight your luggage will be re-checked after customs.

General airport information for McCarran International:
Tel: (702) 261 5211.
www.mccarran.com

Children and age limits

You must be over 21 to gamble and drink alcohol, and these rules are strictly enforced. Under-21s are also prohibited from loitering around casino areas, but there are several activities and centres for this age group along with babysitting facilities and childcare facilities for younger children.

Climate

Las Vegas has an arid climate, with average humidity around 29 per cent and 320 days of desert sunshine each year. In the winter after the sun sets, or even in the shadows, Las Vegas can be quite cold, so take a jacket or extra layer. The same applies when visiting hotels.

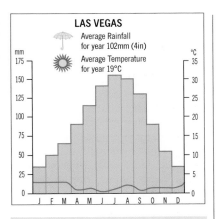

LAS VEGAS

Average Rainfall for year 102mm (4in)

Average Temperature for year 19°C

Weather Conversion Chart
25.4mm = 1 inch
°F = 1.8 x °C + 32

The air conditioning inside the resorts can seem very cold compared to the heat outside, so take an extra layer or you may be forced back outside to warm up.

Consulates

Australia: *150 East 42nd St, 34th Floor, New York, NY 10017-5612.*
Tel: (212) 351 6500.
Canada: *200 South Biscayne Blvd, Suite 1600, Miami, FL 33131.*
Tel: (305) 579 1600.
Republic of Ireland: *Ireland House, 345 Park Ave, 17th Floor, New York, NY 10154-0037.*
Tel: (212) 319 2555.
UK: *SunTrust Center, Suite 2110, 200 South Orange Ave, Orlando, FL 32801.*
Tel: (407) 581 1540.

Conversion tables

See p186

TRAVEL BASICS

Las Vegas is Pacific Standard Time (GMT minus 8 hours).

- Electricity. The power supply is 110/120 volts AC. You will need a US mains adapter and it is preferable to use dual-voltage electric razors and similar devices. There are hairdryers in most hotel rooms.

- You can post international mail from centres in most hotels. See the Yellow Pages for a main post office if you need one.

- Clean public toilets or restrooms can be found in all hotels and establishments throughout the city.

- Take ID. You may need a photo ID to use your credit card or prove that you are over 21. It is not advisable to take your passport around everywhere with you, but a photocard driving licence would be ideal.

Crime prevention and safety

Do not carry more cash than you will need. Store valuables, travel documents and passports in the safe in your hotel room, if there is one available, or ask at the hotel desk for a safety deposit box.

If you have been lucky enough to win at the tables, try not to draw too much attention to your cash bonus. If you win a large amount ask the cashier for a cheque. They can also supply security if you feel it is needed. Security is high in the casinos and on the Strip, and it is generally safe for tourists, but take all the precautions that you would in any major city and do not flaunt jewellery or valuables.

McCarran baggage claim in a quiet moment

If you are driving, avoid using dark hotel car parks at night and use the hotel main entrances, particularly if you are a woman travelling alone. Place valuables out of sight and locked in the trunk (boot).

If you think someone is following you contact hotel security immediately. The same applies if you think there has been an unauthorised entry to your hotel room. Always ensure that your hotel room is locked when you leave it and immediately report any theft or mugging to the police.

When you arrive in your hotel room, make sure you read the fire evacuation notice on the inside of the door and ensure you are aware of where the emergency exits are located. The huge Vegas resorts are easy to get lost in at the best of times, so you do not want any added confusion in an emergency.

There are many street canvassers in Las Vegas, and the best advice is to ignore them. Their material may offend you but their actions rarely pose a threat to visitors. If you want to give money to people begging on the street, the choice is yours, but your money may be better spent if you donate it to a street charity.

Despite the adult themes in Vegas, prostitution is illegal.

Customs regulations

Hand your customs declaration form to Customs. It should list all things brought into the USA, whether gifts for others or not. There is no limit to the amount of cash or traveller's cheques you may bring in or take out. Prohibited items include fresh meat, fruit, drugs (other than prescribed) and plants. Regulations are currently under review – check before leaving. Duty-free allowances for travellers aged 21 or more: 200 cigarettes, 100 cigars and 1 litre of spirits. Travellers aged 18–21: no spirits allowed.

Driving in Las Vegas

You must be over 25 years of age to rent a car in Las Vegas. There are kiosks at the airport but beware of hidden taxes charged on this type of rental. Booking a car before you leave home, or from your hotel, or from a rental depot away from the airport, will be cheaper.

You will need a driving licence and credit card to book a car. Be aware that if you visit Las Vegas during peak season, or when there is a special event or leading convention in town, car availability may be just as scarce as accommodation.

There are free parking facilities in most hotels, but even if valet parking is free you should pay a couple of dollars gratuity. Unless you use the back roads to all the Strip hotels you may find yourself caught up in constant traffic on Las Vegas Boulevard. The worst places to cross the

Check-in desks at Paris

Always ensure that you drink plenty of water

Strip are Tropicana Avenue, Spring Mountain Road and Sahara Avenue, which connect with Interstate 15, so avoid these intersections. The Desert Inn Road is the easiest way to cross the city.

Pay attention to speed limits and wear your seat belt at all times.

National/Statewide car rental companies
Avis. *Tel: (800) 831 2847. www.avis.com*
Dollar. *Tel: (800) 800 4000.*
www.dollar.com
Hertz. *Tel: (800) 654 3131.*
www.hertz.com

Las Vegas car rental companies
Aladdin Rent-A-Car. *Tel: (702) 891 0807.*
Enterprise Rent-A-Car. *Tel: (702) 795 8842. www.enterprise.com*
US Rent-A-Car. *Tel: (702) 798 6100.*
www.us-rentacar.com
X-Press International. *Tel: (702) 736 2663. www.xpressrac.com*

Electricity
The standard electricity supply is 110 volts (60 cycles). You may have to bring an adaptor to convert. Sockets take plugs with two flat pins. Appliances without dual voltage capability will also need a transformer. If in doubt, ask at your hotel.

Emergencies and emergency phone numbers
In an emergency, phone *911*, then ask for the service you require.

Health
Although Las Vegas is a thriving metropolitan city, it is still in the middle of the desert and you may take time to acclimatise to the heat. Drink plenty of water and always ensure you carry water with you while you are walking around. The most cost-effective way of buying water is in drugstores such as Walgreen's or in supermarkets. It can be very

expensive in hotel food outlets and bars. The water in your hotel room is filtered and safe to drink but not pleasant. If you drink alcohol your chances of dehydration are severely increased. Make sure that your skin is not exposed to the sun. Cover up with light clothing, wear plenty of sunscreen and bring sunglasses. Sun can easily penetrate through clouds so do not be fooled by overcast weather. The air is extremely dry, so wear lip balm, take advantage of the free moisturisers supplied with the toiletries in your hotel room, and contact lens wearers should bring extra solution.

Bring comfortable shoes as you could find yourself walking miles as you explore the Strip. If you have any difficulties walking, you will also want to ensure that your hotel room is conveniently located close to a lift. With the combination of the dry desert air and construction in this growing city, travellers with asthma or allergies to dust may be severely affected and you may not be able to stay in Vegas more than a few days before it gets the better of you. Hay fever may also be a problem, particularly if you have an allergy to sagebrush.

Before you leave, make sure that you have medical insurance cover for at least $1 million. Take a credit card, as you will have to pay a fee to visit a doctor and may incur pharmaceutical costs on top. You will have to claim these expenses back from your insurance company

Hotel reception of the Four Seasons

Conversion Table

FROM	TO	MULTIPLY BY
Inches	Centimetres	2.54
Feet	Metres	0.3048
Yards	Metres	0.9144
Miles	Kilometres	1.6090
Acres	Hectares	0.4047
Gallons	Litres	4.5460
Ounces	Grams	28.35
Pounds	Grams	453.6
Pounds	Kilograms	0.4536
Tons	Tonnes	1.0160

To convert back, for example from centimetres to inches, divide by the number in the third column.

Men's Suits

UK		36	38	40	42	44	46	48
Rest of Europe	46	48	50	52	54	56	58
USA		36	38	40	42	44	46	48

Dress Sizes

UK		8	10	12	14	16	18
France		36	38	40	42	44	46
Italy		38	40	42	44	46	48
Rest of Europe	34	36	38	40	42	44
USA		6	8	10	12	14	16

Men's Shirts

UK	14	14.5	15	15.5	16	16.5	17
Rest of Europe	36	37	38	39/40	41	42	43
USA	14	14.5	15	15.5	16	16.5	17

Men's Shoes

UK		7	7.5	8.5	9.5	10.5	11
Rest of Europe	41	42	43	44	45	46
USA		8	8.5	9.5	10.5	11.5	12

Women's Shoes

UK		4.5	5	5.5	6	6.5	7
Rest of Europe	38	38	39	39	40	41
USA		6	6.5	7	7.5	8	8.5

when you return, so keep all your receipts. If the treatment is serious and likely to be expensive you will need to contact your insurance company directly, so make sure you take all the appropriate details and contact numbers with you.

If you are on any prescribed medication do not forget to take it with you on your trip and ensure that the supply will last for the length of your stay.

Medical help and emergencies

If you are taken ill, contact your hotel desk for information, or call a visiting doctor:
Inn-House Doctor Inc.
Tel: (702) 259 1616.
Nevada Resort Medical Services.
Tel: (702) 893 6767.
IN AN EMERGENCY CALL 911.

Money matters

The unit of currency in the United States is the US Dollar ($), which is made up from 100 cents (¢).

Common coin denominations are:

1¢	Penny
5¢	Nickel
10¢	Dime
25¢	Quarter (meaning quarter dollar)

50¢ and $1 coins are also available, but are rare. Notes come in $1, $5, $10, $20, $50 and $100 denominations, but they are all the same size and colour so be careful not to mix them up. Higher notes are also available but are not readily accepted in most shops or establishments.

Most hotels will exchange your foreign currency and there are several exchange bureaus in Las Vegas. It is advisable to bring traveller's cheques, which should be in US dollars. Traveller's cheques will be accepted as cash in most establishments (with photo ID) and most hotels or banks will exchange them for you, although taxi drivers will not accept them as payment. You will often need photo ID to use your credit card. Most major credit cards such as AMEX, Carte Blanche, Diners Club, Discover, MasterCard (Eurocard, Chargex) and VISA (Barclaycard) will be accepted in Las Vegas. For a fee, you can also get a cash advance on your credit card, but it is more cost-effective to withdraw cash from an ATM. You will find points in most hotels, where you will be charged a small fee to your account but will benefit from a lower exchange rate.

Pedestrians

Take extra care when crossing the Strip. There are six lanes of busy traffic and

More city landmarks in New York–New York Hotel and Casino

drivers are often distracted by the many sights on Las Vegas Boulevard. Cross the Strip at pedestrian crossing points or use the bridges. Remember that traffic will be moving on the right-hand side of the road and take care when walking across hotel entrances, as cars may be turning into them. Only cross roads when the 'WALK' symbol is displayed at pedestrian crossings and walk swiftly – you only have a short time to cross those six lanes.

Pharmacies

There are pharmacy counters in most supermarkets and drugstores. Walgreen's is conveniently located on the Strip, north of the Fashion Show Mall between Desert Inn Road and Convention Center Drive. *Walgreen Drug Stores, 3030 Las Vegas Blvd S. Tel: (702) 642 1901.*

Sustainable travel

Thomas Cook is a strong advocate of ethical and fairly traded tourism and believes that the travel experience should be as good for the places visited as it is for the people who visit them. That's why we

US mailbox

The Luxor light beam is visible from space

firmly support The Travel Foundation, a charity that develops solutions to help improve and protect holiday destinations, their environment, traditions and culture. To find out what you can do to make a positive difference to the places you travel to and the people who live there, please visit *www.thetravelfoundation.org.uk*

Telephones

To dial a local number ignore the area code (702 in brackets) and dial the remaining seven digits directly. If you are calling from a hotel room you may have to enter a number to get an outside line before you dial. See the instructions printed on the top of your telephone.

For national calls and Canada, add a 1 before the area code (in brackets). For international calls dial 011 followed by the country code (for example 44 for the UK), then the area code (omitting the 0), then the local number.

Country codes

Australia *61*	**France** *33*
Germany *49*	**Ireland** *353*
Netherlands *31*	**Spain** *34*
UK *44*	

If you are calling overseas from a public phone box, you will need at least $5–$6 in quarters and the operator may need to connect you. The operator can be reached by dialling 0.

In hotels and casinos, public phone boxes are usually found by the toilets (or restrooms). They can also be found outside supermarkets and petrol stations and inside restaurants. Calling from your hotel room can be extremely expensive, even for national calls.

If you want to use your mobile phone in the United States, check with your service provider that your phone is suitable and your service plan covers overseas travel. They will also advise you on the costs of these calls, which may be high. You can hire mobile phones when you visit: they are often available at car rental depots or your hotel can locate one for you. Again, calls will be costly.

The most economical way of making calls from a hotel room or public phone box is to use an international calling card. Hotel stores, drugstores and supermarkets sell them and they are usually available at most airports, but if you buy one before leaving home it will give you the opportunity to find the most cost-effective and suitable card for your visit.

Business services and internet access

Most hotels have business centres, which can provide fax, photocopying or internet facilities. You may also be able to access the internet from your hotel room. There are several internet cafés and access centres in Las Vegas, which usually charge between $5 and $12 per half-hour.

Tourist information

For tourist information, entertainment schedules and money-saving coupons there are several free magazines available throughout Las Vegas such as *Las Vegas Today*, *Showbiz*, *Vegas Visitor* and *What's On*. The two main daily newspapers are the *Las Vegas Sun* and the *Las Vegas Review Journal*.

Las Vegas Information Centre, 3150 Paradise Road.
Tel: (702) 892 7575.
www.visitlasvegas.com

Other useful websites:
www.travelnevada.com
www.vegas.com

Travellers with disabilities

Las Vegas is a very accessible city for people in wheelchairs. If you have any specific accommodation needs, your hotel will be happy to help you in your booking. Most showrooms have assisted-listening devices and wheelchair access, as do restaurants and casinos, with slot machines at easy reach. Many airport shuttles are equipped with lifting devices, and if you are hiring a car you can obtain a disabled parking permit from the City of Las Vegas Parking Permit Office, *tel: (702) 229 6431*, in advance.

ACKNOWLEDGEMENTS

Thomas Cook Publishing wishes to thank ETHEL DAVIES for the photographs reproduced in this book, to whom the copyright in the photographs belongs, with the exception of the following:

Cirque du Soleil (photo Tomasz Rossa, costumes Dominique Lemieux) 124, 131; Harrahs Las Vegas Public Relations 78; Las Vegas News Bureau 6, 8, 10, 12, 16, 17, 22a, 23, 24b, 25, 30, 31a, 31b, 38a, 38b, 48, 51, 53, 56, 57, 58b, 67, 72, 82, 98, 123, 126, 129, 144, 154b, 155, 164, 167, 168b, 169; MGM Mirage 44a, 44b, 51, 132, 146a; Pictures Colour Library 40b, 46a, 56a, 88a, 88b, 158b, 159, 160; Venetian Hotel 77, 140; Wayne Bernath 64

Index: INDEXING SPECIALISTS (UK) LTD

Maps: PC GRAPHICS, Old Woking, UK

Proof-reading: JAN McCANN for CAMBRIDGE PUBLISHING MANAGEMENT LTD

Send your thoughts to
books@thomascook.com

We're committed to providing the very best up-to-date information in our travel guides and constantly strive to make them as useful as they can be. You can help us to improve future editions by letting us have your feedback. If you've made a wonderful discovery on your travels that we don't already feature, if you'd like to inform us about recent changes to anything that we do include, or if you simply want to let us know your thoughts about this guidebook and how we can make it even better – we'd love to hear from you.

Send us ideas, discoveries and recommendations today and then look out for your valuable input in the next edition of this title. And, as an extra 'thank you' from Thomas Cook Publishing, you'll be automatically entered into our exciting monthly prize draw.

Emails to the above address, or letters to Travellers Project Editor, Thomas Cook Publishing, PO Box 227, Unit 18, Coningsby Road, Peterborough PE3 8SB, UK.

Please don't forget to let us know which title your feedback refers to!